DATE			

INTERIOR DESIGN
ON YOUR OWN

INTERIOR DESIGN

ON YOUR OWN

The Complete Guide to Home Decorating

JILL BLAKE

AND THE EDITORS OF CONSUMER REPORTS BOOKS

CONSUMER REPORTS BOOKS

A DIVISION OF CONSUMERS UNION

Yonkers, New York

Copyright 1986 by Quarto Publishing Ltd.

Copyright © 1993 by Quarto Publishing plc and
Consumers Union of United States, Inc.,
Yonkers, New York 10703.

Published by Consumers Union of United States, Inc.,
Yonkers, New York 10703.

Library of Congress Cataloging-in-Publication Data

Blake, Jill.
Interior design on your own : the complete guide to home
decorating / Jill Blake and the editors of Consumer Reports Books.—
1st American ed.
p.   cm.
Includes index.
ISBN 0-89043-638-X
1. Interior decoration—Handbooks, manuals, etc.   I. Consumer
Reports Books.   II. Title.
NK2115.B55 1993   93-22727
747—dc20   CIP

First published in Great Britain in 1986
as How to Solve Your Interior Design Problems by Jill Blake.

Illustrations by Ray Brown, Mulkern Rutherford Studios, and Fraser Newman

Design by Ruth Kolbert

First American Edition

First printing, October 1993

Manufactured in the United States of America

Printed on recycled paper

INTERIOR DESIGN ON YOUR OWN is a Consumer Reports Book published by Consumers Union, the nonprofit organization that publishes *Consumer Reports,* the monthly magazine of test reports, product Ratings, and buying guidance. Established in 1936, Consumers Union is chartered under the Not-for-Profit Corporation Law of the State of New York. The purposes of Consumers Union, as stated in its charter, are to provide consumers with information and counsel on consumer goods and services, to give information on all matters relating to the expenditure of the family income, and to initiate and to cooperate with individual and group efforts seeking to create and maintain decent living standards.

Acknowledgments

Special thanks to Joan Vos MacDonald,
the photo researcher on this book,
and to Jill Herbers for her editorial assistance.

Contents

SECTION FOUR
A SENSE OF STYLE

SECTION FIVE
DIRECTORY OF MATERIALS

INTRODUCTION

WHETHER YOUR HOME IS LARGE OR SMALL, PERIOD OR contemporary, in the country or in the city, getting the tone and style right is vital. Interior design and decoration involve not just questions of choosing color schemes, selecting different styles, and ordering fabulous furnishings. Also important in designing and decorating rooms is that they be practical as well as good-looking. Selecting schemes that enhance or complement the appearance and mood of a room, and above all, creating a pleasant and satisfying living environment that is tailored to meet your needs are also essential.

Most homes have their problems, whether structural or superficial. *Interior Design on Your Own* offers advice on color selection, room planning, lighting, furniture, and window dressing for every room. It shows you how to alter visually the shape and proportions of awkward rooms, and how to enhance good features and disguise bad ones. Achieving the desired atmosphere involves careful planning, but it is surprisingly easy to correct early mistakes, rescue a color scheme that just doesn't work, and even rectify a structural or design disaster. Simply adding, regrouping, or highlighting well-chosen accents and accessories can make a world of difference. There is also practical advice on choosing and using paint, wall coverings, floorings, tiles, fabrics, and soft furnishings.

Interior Design on Your Own is a practical manual. Use it to help plan new design schemes and to identify and deal with problem features. The book is divided into five sections. Section One: Design Analysis outlines the principles of interior design and should be used in conjunction with all the following sections. Section Two: Design in Practice deals with the specific interior design requirements of each room/area in the home, and with lighting and window treatments. Section Three: Design Renewal offers practical solutions to built-in design problems and covers renovating bad surfaces and disguising awkwardly shaped rooms. Section Four: A Sense of Style analyzes the decorating and design elements that make up popular styles, such as Country, Victorian, or Eclectic. Section Five: Directory of Materials is a reference section showing the available types of paint, fabric, wall covering, flooring, and lighting fixtures, and indicating their suitability for different interior design purposes.

The secret of design success lies in being able to look at the rooms in your home

objectively. You will have to decide whether you should throw out all the existing
furniture and furnishings and start again, or take what you already have and add to it.
This book is designed to help you bring out the best in what you've got, with the hope
that the many illustrations, descriptions, and suggestions will inspire you to be a little
bolder, more daring, perhaps even unconventional, in the way you decorate and
furnish your home.

SECTION ONE

DESIGN ANALYSIS

NO SUCCESSFUL PLANNING, FURNISHING, AND interior design idea can exist in a vacuum, no color scheme can be dreamed up in total isolation. Ideas have to relate to an actual room, taking into account its size, shape, atmosphere, and positive and negative features. Its purpose and function have to be considered, together with the life-style of the people who use it.

Any good professional interior designer will spend time talking to clients to find out exactly what sort of design they require. Professionals will often deliberate for a long time over personal taste in this regard, and they know how hard it is to come to a well-thought-out final decision. There is no point in producing a beautiful show house that no one wants to live in; a satisfied client is one who really enjoys living in his or her redesigned home. The secret of successful interior design is to reconcile all the necessary items of furniture within the basic shell while, at the same time, creating a pleasing, harmonious environment.

Translating your ideas into reality can sometimes be the most difficult part of the design process, and it may only be possible to make final decisions, even decisions that alter the original plans, while work is in progress. You might discover structural obstacles and have to accommodate them. You might decide that the color of the paint for the woodwork or walls is not the shade you intended. It is not until you start working on large expanses that you can really see the overall effect of your efforts. Remember, however, that newly decorated walls, ceilings, and woodwork can be transformed by the finishing touches of fabric, floor coverings, and furniture. Maintaining a flexible approach to your design and making minor adjustments as you go along is one of the keys to success.

Getting the Framework Right

Basically, you should think of a room as a box, however irregularly shaped, and then break it down into its component parts. You will need to decide on suitable surface treatments and textures, as well as an overall color scheme. Consider furniture and shelving or storage, any practical equipment such as bathroom fixtures and kitchen appliances, window treatments, and lighting and styling accessories.

ASSESS THE ROOM

Look at the room critically. Study its size and shape and any existing advantages it may have. Then consider any negative aspects or disadvantages. You should aim to capitalize on the good points, enhance the attractive features, and play down weak points. However, if you cannot disguise obtrusive features, you can sometimes make them more interesting by emphasizing them creatively.

ATMOSPHERE

Decide on the mood or atmosphere you want the room to have—warm, cool, elegant, spacious, intimate, stimulating, restful. The type of atmosphere you want will dictate the basic choice of colors.

STYLE

When thinking about style there are many possibilities to consider, ranging from rustic to elegant, traditional to modern, with all the variations in between. The style you select may depend on the intrinsic architectural quality of the building. It is safer to echo and enhance its natural character than to try to disguise or compete with it. A turn-of-the-century Victorian house would look uncomfortable decorated in the sleek chrome and leather style of modern design, for example. The starting point for selecting a style may come from a cherished heirloom, a special collection of accessories, or a particular design in the pattern of a carpet, wall covering, or upholstery fabric.

It does not take a design expert to give a dull, boxlike room character and atmosphere, but to match a good idea in theory with success in practice, you need to identify each aspect of a proposed design and understand how all the elements should come together.

Start a collection of samples, catalogs, and pictures that reflect your ideal scheme or suggest different approaches to design for particular rooms. Do not buy materials or items of furniture at this stage.

BASIC PLAN

Work out a plan on paper. Whatever the purpose and function of the room, it will contain furniture. It may need storage facilities and have to incorporate equipment and electrical and plumbing devices. The way to work it all out to be sure everything will fit in and that

This set of before-and-after photographs shows how the owners of this seaside California condominium considered the positive and negative aspects of their new home and designed accordingly. To give the sky and sea center stage, the owners decided to dispense with curtains and louver the windows. Curtains would have made a small room seem even smaller; louvers provide shade and privacy without obscuring the view. A wall-size mirror covers the wall surrounding the fireplace, both to reflect the sky and to create an illusion of space. Accenting a basic black-and-white color scheme are colors found in sunsets.

you have the best possible arrangement is on an accurate floor plan.

Another option is new computer software that allows you to see room designs, complete with walls, appliances, and furniture, in color and three-dimensionally. All the elements of the room can be moved around on-screen to try out different arrangements.

APPRAISE THE EFFECTS

Check your design plan carefully. Once you have an idea of the range of materials you might want to use, obtain larger samples that home design centers are now offering. Look at them in the room, both in daylight and at night in the artificial light under which they will be viewed. Floor coverings are seen both horizontally and from above and work surfaces are seen at waist level. Wall coverings and tiles are seen vertically, both with the light shining directly on them and in shadow. The same wall treatment can look totally different in two areas of the same room if the lighting conditions are varied.

USING EXPERT HELP

When you have planned the overall scheme and have chosen materials, you may have to call in professionals to help you complete the design. The effect you want to achieve could involve, for example, new plumbing and electrical work, carpenters for fitting furniture, or simply the aid of an interior decorator to put the design together. You might even need an architect if structural changes are involved.

An emerging specialist today is the space designer, a licensed professional whose role falls somewhere between an architect and an interior designer. A space designer can make valuable suggestions and structural decisions about moving walls and reorganizing rooms so that full use is made of their design potential. By means of seemingly straightforward changes, he or she can help you visualize rooms that can work in entirely different ways.

Before making any decisions, get estimates from three or four recommended professionals so you can compare prices and estimate the amount of time the work is likely to take.

Measuring Up

Before you can plan a room or fit in any furniture or appliances, you need to take accurate measurements. The most original design ideas can go wrong if the measurements are even a fraction off.

Measure everything and double-check your figures. Don't forget to take a yardstick or steel measuring tape with you to jot down measurements when you shop for new items.

Draw a rough sketch of the basic shape of the room. Measure and mark in windows, doors, recesses, and projections. Also mark in any fixed items, such as radiators and heating ducts, electrical outlets, telephone jacks, built-in furniture, and plumbing pipes and outlets. Measure the width and height of doorjambs, window frames and sills, baseboards, cornices, chair rails (decorative moldings installed around a room at chair level), friezes, and fireplaces.

CALCULATING DIMENSIONS

Work out the total floor or ceiling area by multiplying the length of the room by the width. Find out the total wall area by multiplying the length of each wall by the height, and adding them all together. You will need these measurements to estimate quantities of paint, wallpaper, and floor coverings. You will also need accurate window measurements to estimate curtain fabric requirements or the size of blinds or shades.

MAKING A SCALED PLAN

Transfer your rough sketch to graph paper to make a plan that is correctly scaled. A useful scale is ½ inch equals 12 inches (1 foot). Using a sharp pencil, draw the perimeter of the room. Indicate the doors, windows, built-in furniture, or wall units, including which direction any of these items open, and all other features to scale. Plot the exact positions of electrical outlets. Ink in the finished plan, leaving any existing elements that you plan to change (for example, bathroom fixtures) outlined in pencil only.

FITTING IN THE FURNITURE

Accurately measure existing or new furniture you plan to use, obtaining the measurements for new pieces from the store or catalog where they're sold. On separate pieces of paper, draw the shapes to the same scale as the room plan. Color-code them—using one color for existing items and another for anticipated purchases—then mark on them what they are and cut them out. This will enable you to try different plans and check to see that things fit.

When you have decided on the best positions for everything, tape the furniture cutouts onto the plan. Remember to allow enough space for people to walk around freestanding furniture, to push chairs back from tables and desks, to open doors and drawers, and to pull beds out for making or cleaning underneath. Both the bathroom and kitchen are areas where free access to fixed units must be carefully thought out. Lighting and any further plumbing changes can then be planned.

THINKING THREE-DIMENSIONALLY

It is often necessary to visualize rooms three-dimensionally. In the kitchen, for example, it is essential to see if work surfaces will fit under windows and whether appliances will fit under or on work surfaces. It may then be necessary to make elevated plans for each wall. Follow the same principles of measuring to scale and fitting in, with the shapes drawn and cut out to the same scale as the wall plan, but in elevation, showing profiles instead of the overall picture. Tape the items into place once you have decided where you want to put them.

A three-dimensional sketch like this is particularly useful in kitchen planning, because it draws attention to potential problem areas, such as surfaces that are too low for comfort or wall units with sharp projecting corners.

$\mathscr{T}$he Basic Shell

Once you have ascertained that the floors, walls, ceilings, and windows are basically sound, you will need to explore all the different materials and treatments available and select the ones that suit your style.

FLOOR

This is usually the largest unbroken area in a room, and although furniture will conceal it to some extent, it is still the most noticeable surface. Although the ceiling is the same size, it does not have the same impact. Floor coverings and surface treatments, therefore, have to be selected carefully if they are to produce the right effect. There are dozens of types of floor treatments, each suited to different needs and preferences:

Hard floorings Materials such as wood, brick, tile, or marble are the most durable and are normally fitted directly onto the subfloor. They stand up to heavy wear and tear and traffic. Some homes already have existing hardwood floors that can be beautifully refinished if they are in good condition.

Semisoft floorings Flooring made of materials such as vinyl and linoleum comes in sheets or individual tiles. It is fairly durable and thick, and "bouncy" underfoot. This type of flooring is relatively easy to clean and maintain, making it perfect for high-traffic areas like kitchens.

Soft floorings Rugs and carpeting come in many types of materials and are frequently laid on top of one of the other kinds of flooring. Some cover the whole floor (wall-to-wall) and are fully fitted, others cover only part of the floor and can be laid anywhere. How long they will last and how easy they are to clean will depend on the type chosen—the fiber from which it is made, the length of pile (if any), and in some cases, the type of backing.

CEILING

Often the ceiling of a room can appear too high or too low. To make a high ceiling appear lower, decorate it in a color and texture similar to the floor. Or paint it a dark color, or at least a shade or two darker than the walls.

To "raise" a low ceiling visually, paint or even paper it a light color, such as a pale sky blue, or a shade or two lighter than what is on the walls.

If a ceiling features decorative cornices and moldings, or perhaps has attractive old beams, try to enhance or restore them. A light color painted on the relief decoration with a darker color on the background or ceiling "bed" will help dramatize the effect of decorative plasterwork. This kind of original craftsmanship is hard to come by today, and it is more than worth the effort to emphasize it and show it off.

Most of the treatments for walls are also suitable for ceilings, including tenting with fabric for a soft look or to hide ceilings with a lot of surface imperfections.

WALLS

Walls form a large proportion of the total surface of a room. They can be used to form a backdrop to accessories or to serve a specific design function of their own. Colored or patterned in different ways, they can visually change the proportions of an awkwardly shaped room; for example, they can make a room appear larger or smaller than it really is.

You will need to select surface treatments and materials to create the right atmosphere and style for the room, at the same time considering other practical aspects. It makes sense, for example, to use washable or vinyl wall coverings or impermeable ceramic tiles in bathrooms, where there is a lot of water and steam, or in kitchens, where grease is prevalent. But delicate, pretty decorations such as tenting the walls and ceiling with fabric should be limited to spaces such as living rooms or bedrooms.

There are three basic ways of treating walls, although there are many variations within each group:

The Natural Look

You may be lucky enough to have walls made of natural materials, such as stone, brick, or wood paneling. These materials alone can set the style of a room by evoking a certain atmosphere. They may need time-consuming cleaning, renovation, and sealing, but they are worth it. If you don't already have such walls, they may be created by placing a stone or brick surface on top of smooth, plastered interiors. You may even discover, by chipping away existing old plaster, natural materials underneath.

Paint

Paint for walls is available in several textures, types, and finishes and can be used decoratively in many different ways. Painting walls is simple, and colors can easily be changed if necessary. There are also various ways of enhancing a painted surface: murals, faux and trompe l'oeil effects, and the special painting techniques of rag rolling, stippling, sponging, and dragging. A stenciled border can highlight an architectural focal point or just run around the walls for a charming effect.

Paint is also used for woodwork and metalwork. These surfaces are often seen as a "trim" to a room, and can be highlighted in contrasting or neutral colors. Alternatively, woodwork can be made unobtrusive by matching or toning it with the color of the walls. Wood can also be stained and sealed, rather than painted, or veneered and polished to blend in with the furniture.

Wall Coverings

Wall coverings are available in a wide variety of types, from conventional wallpapers to tiles and fabrics. Some, such as textured wall coverings, more easily disguise a poor, badly plastered surface than do others. Start with a good, smooth wall if you plan to use reflective or delicately textured wall coverings. Some coverings, such as easy-peel wallpapers and vinyls, are very easy to hang and to remove. They can also be painted or papered over later. Other types, such as ceramic tiles, heavy relief wall coverings, and wood panels, are semipermanent and sometimes difficult to remove. Think ahead about changes you might want to make the next

The moment of truth! Stripped walls, bare floorboards, and uncurtained windows are easier to comprehend. You can see exactly how to improve or enhance the basic structure and what visual tricks to play either to alter the size and shape of the room or to emphasize or disguise an integral feature such as a fireplace or door. You may have planned the color scheme; selected patterns, texture, and surface treatments; and decided on designs and furniture before the room was stripped back to the raw. Reconsider these plans carefully and be prepared to change them.

*   Any of the styles illustrated in Section Four could be imposed on this room. You can be guided by the architectural features or you can alter them completely.*

Ceiling

Consider replastering or lining with paper, lighting (this is the time to dig out channels for wiring), retaining or removing cornices, decoration.

Walls

Consider replastering exposed brick and poorly plastered areas, wiring for outlets, wall lights, and speakers; retaining or removing the picture rail (perhaps with the cornices the effect is overelaborate); lining walls before painting or papering with texture.

Windows

Consider stripping back and sanding window frames; replacing stained glass in upper section; window treatments (maximize light coming into room by hanging curtains clear of glass).

Fireplace

Consider excavating or installing a period or modern fireplace or mantel, depending on scheme.

Floor

Consider refurbishing floorboards and replacing as necessary; sanding smooth, staining, and sealing or covering.

time around and allow for this when selecting a wall treatment.

FURNITURE

Whether freestanding or built-in, furniture must suit the style, purpose, and function of a room. Again, choose the actual surface of the furniture—natural wood, highly polished or inlaid wood, laminate or upholstery fabrics—with care, making sure it fits your needs.

Size is just as important as style, so think spatially when buying or ordering furniture. Avoid crowding a small room with too many pieces. Put striking items in a large room or group them to make focal points. Take height into account—high-ceilinged rooms look good furnished with several tall pieces. You could use built-in bookcases or cabinets in a living room, for example, or have a dominating headboard or four-poster bed in a bedroom. Refer to your measurements to work out the right scale relationships between room size and furniture.

ACCENTS AND ACCESSORIES

The accents and furnishing accessories that complete a design are all part of dressing the basic shell of a room. They can add character and style as well as bring a dull color scheme to life, or provide the necessary link to the visual cohesion of a room.

Accessories are anything that embellishes a room, from pictures, prints, and wall hangings to mirrors, displays of books and collectibles, and groupings of houseplants. Glass, china, pottery, and colorful cushion arrangements can be added to living areas, innovative and stylish equipment and cooking utensils to kitchens, and high-design linens and towels to bathrooms. Table and standard lamps, lamp shades, and light fixtures are accessories, but the larger problem of lighting itself will be discussed later.

Color, Pattern, and Texture

Color, pattern, and texture are the surface elements of interior design that can be manipulated to produce different effects of space, scale, and shape, whatever the basic structures of a room and its furnishings. The decisions you make, whether they be colors for walls and ceilings or textural details in small finishing touches, determine the impression you want to create with the overall scheme.

These three surface qualities are closely linked. In decorating, you have to deal with the givens of a room. The smoothness of plastered walls is totally different from the feel of wooden window frames and doors. These qualities are absolutely fundamental, even if you do no more than use the simplest of color schemes to paint the room. You can also choose to add pattern and texture, for emphasis or concealment. Whether you employ paint, fabric, paper, or other such materials to create an effect, every decision adds another element that plays an active part. Each choice may modify previous choices.

COLOR: A BASIC APPROACH

Any color scheme needs to be related to a specific room—its purpose and function, the number and type of people who are going to use it, and the mood and atmosphere you want to create in it. If you are working within a careful budget and have to incorporate existing items or forgo expensive decorating

and finishing materials, you can still be inventive with the color scheme.

The lighting, too, can work some miraculous color changes and be used to emphasize good features and play down unattractive ones.

An Eye for Color

Color makes an immediate visual impact and creates a mood. It is the first thing people notice about a room, although they may not consciously relate the atmosphere to the color scheme. When visitors remark how warm, cozy, rich, inviting, cool, elegant, spacious, or intimate a room is, the colors used have helped create these impressions. In fact, color itself is an illusion created by the way the eye receives and the brain interprets light. It is these illusory qualities that make color such a useful design tool.

Think of sunlight, pure white light. Pass this light through a prism, and you see the entire spectrum, all the colors of the rainbow. Every object we see has a surface composition that absorbs light and reflects back only part of the spectrum, so what we see as a red object is one that absorbs all the other colors and reflects back only the red light. This is why colors appear to change under different kinds of illumination.

The colors we see all around us can best be described in two categories: the colors of nature—seen in such things as the sky, flowers, foliage, animals, and birds—and artificial colors—those in which synthetic pigments and dyes are used in special formulas to create paints, inks, fabric dyes, and so forth. There are literally thousands of possible colors and color combinations in the decorator's palette.

Working with Color

A little understanding of color theory will help you work with color creatively. One of the best ways of learning about it is by looking at a color wheel (see below). The pigment and dye spectrum relates to the *primary colors*—red, yellow, and blue. All the other colors originate from these three entirely pure colors, which cannot be created from any combination of other pigments. By using two primary colors together, you get a *secondary color*. There are three secondaries, corresponding to the three primaries: orange (red and yellow), green (blue and yellow) and vi-

olet (red and blue). These six colors make up the basic spectrum. The primaries and secondaries can be paired together to create *complementary colors*: red and green, blue and orange, yellow and violet. Each pair demonstrates the strongest possible contrast between colors, since the secondary color contains no trace of its complementary. If you stare at a strong color fixedly for a few moments, then blink or look away, you will see the complementary color as an afterimage.

The color wheel can be further subdivided into *tertiary colors*. These are made by mixing together equal parts of a primary color and the secondary color adjacent to it on the color wheel, creating red-orange, yellow-orange, yellow-green, blue-green, blue-violet, and red-violet. These are all pure colors and are called *hues*.

All the colors on one side of the wheel are

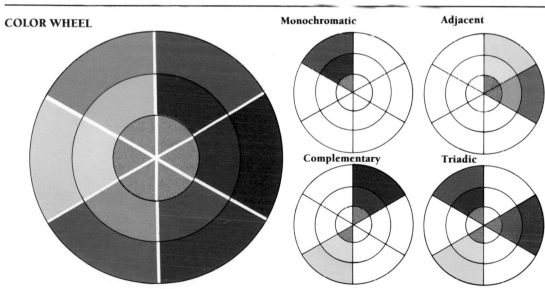

COLOR WHEEL

Monochromatic

Adjacent

Complementary

Triadic

The color wheel shows pure hues on the outer edge— **primary** *colors of red, yellow, and blue, with* **secondary** *colors of orange, green, and violet or purple. The middle circle shows* **tints,** *formed by mixing these colors with white to make them lighter. The inner circle shows* **shades** *made by mixing black with the pure color to darken and enrich. Basic color schemes*

include: **monochromatic**—*made by using shades, tints, and pure hues of any one color;* **contemporary**—*made by using two colors that face each other on the wheel;* **adjacent**—*made by using three or four colors next to each other on the color wheel;* **triadic**—*made by using three equidistant colors.*

Color creates atmosphere and mood. Choosing patterns and textures sets the style. This gregarious living room owes its warmth and charm as much to its rosy reds, apricots, tans, and greens as it does to its comfortable furniture and conversation-inspiring collectibles. The walls' golden color gives the room a sunny glow that compensates for a lack of direct sunlight. A painted screen decorated with green tendrils complements the vivid floral pattern on the couches. Texture is varied and abundant, including the sisal rug, rough-hewn miniature houses, ethnic knitted pillows, and a basketful of hydrangeas.

"warm" colors: red-violet, red, red-orange, orange, yellow-orange, yellow. Those on the other side are "cool": green, blue-green, blue, blue-violet. All the warm colors are *advancing* or dominant colors, that is, they appear to come toward you. Strong, warm colors used in a room can make it seem cozy and intimate, but if too many bright, advancing colors are used in a small room, the effect can be claustrophobic or extremely garish.

All the cool colors are *receding*—they ap-

pear to go away from you. They can help to create an illusion of space, particularly if the pale tones of the colors are used. If equal quantities of a warm and cool color are used together in a room, the warmer color will appear to predominate. Two colors fall at the junction of cool and warm: yellow-green and violet. Their quality depends on their relationship to the warm or cool color.

As well as tints and shades (see color wheels) there are the *neutrals*. In interior de-

In contrast, the corner of this bedroom in a seaside condominium is a place for quiet private moments. The surprisingly easy-on-the-eye black-and-white scheme is accented only by gray-and-pink pillows. Texture is subtly varied, from the nubby weave of the chair to the soft nap of the rug. This room is passive. It waits for Pacific sunsets to provide spectacular color and lets the sunlight through the louvered windows create its own patterns.

sign, these include the full range of gray, brown, beige, cream, and off-white tones. Strictly speaking, however, the only true neutrals are a pure gray, produced by mixing together equal quantities of the three primary colors or black and white. All the other so-

called neutrals relate back to the colors on the wheel: Browns can tend toward red or green; gray can be gray-green, blue-gray, or lilac-gray; beige can be tinged with pink, blue, yellow, or green; and each tint in the entire range of off-whites has a starting point in the spectrum. This is why color matching has to be done just as carefully with neutrals and pastels as with the bolder, brighter hues.

Harmony and Contrast

When it comes to planning color for interior decoration, there are two basic types of schemes. One consists of harmonious or *related* colors and the other of contrasting or *complementary* colors.

A harmonious scheme uses adjacent colors on the wheel (sometimes called "analogous" colors) or a monochromatic theme (tone on tone) with various values of the same color from light to dark. Great care is needed when creating a monochromatic scheme to ensure noticeable contrast between the tones, or it may seem dull. The simplest monochrome range is based on a single segment of the color wheel. It is rarely successful to mix pure colors with secondaries and tertiaries made from the same color.

Harmonious color schemes are usually easy to live with and tend to create a relaxed atmosphere. They make a useful background for patterned upholstery fabrics, since the colors do not compete with them or with one another.

Contrasting or complementary schemes are created by using colors opposite each other on the wheel—for example, red with green or blue with orange. Contrasting color schemes are more exciting than harmonious ones; they can be highly stimulating and are rarely restful.

A *split-complementary scheme* occurs when three colors equidistant on the wheel are combined—as with the three primaries of red, yellow, and blue, or with red-orange, yellow-green, and blue-violet. A scheme involving a fourth distinct hue is called a *tetrad*.

Color theory helps to explain the behavior of color and the relationships of different hues. But there are modifying factors that must be used in your planning, especially when it comes to dealing with paint, fabric, and paper, and with space, mass, and light. The pigments and dyes that create the colors of different materials do not conform absolutely to the theory of color. Some pigments, for example, are impure and devalue a color mixture, while others dominate weaker colors. Black or strong red will flood out a paint mixture rather than enrich it. The same color dyed into fabric and painted on the wall will have different qualities in each case. The color of paint is modified by a glossy or matte finish and may alter as the paint dries. Here again, it is important to have samples of all the actual materials and to observe the effect in the setting itself.

Putting Theory into Practice

To translate your color ideas into reality, start once again with the basic features of a room: its shape, size, and intrinsic atmosphere. Consider also the amount of natural daylight it receives. If a room is cold, you can use mainly warm colors. These can be light, dark, rich, or strong, depending on the size of the room. If you want to make it seem more spacious, use pastel colors: pale pink, peach, apricot, pastel yellow, warm beige, cream. If it is a large room, it will support stronger values: pure red, orange, and yellow. If it is dark as well as cold, create a sunny impression by using lots of yellow and yellow-orange teamed with sparkling white or vibrant orange, set off against a smooth cream.

If the room is warm and has plenty of light, it will look elegant decorated in the cooler colors: blue, green, lilac, blue-violet, cool gray, and black and white. Again, if it is a large area, you can use stronger hues, but if it is small and you want to create an illusion of space, use the very palest values from the cool side of the wheel. A restrained, cool, monochromatic scheme creates the most spacious impression of all.

Many schemes benefit from some neutral touches, to act as a contrast or a link. Neutrals are often chosen for the ceiling, as the background to fabric, or for the floor area, but neutrals need not always be used in this way. They can play an integral part in the design or be used to construct a whole scheme, creating a restrained, elegant atmosphere.

In order to emphasize a scheme and highlight its basically warm or cool character, add a few contrasting accents from the opposite side of the color wheel.

Alternatively, use accents for tonal contrast. If a room is decorated mainly in cool pale greens, add some rich terra-cotta or rose accents, or for a really vibrant effect, red or orange. If it is schemed in rich, dark blues, choose soft pink, peach, or apricot, or sunshine or primrose yellow. In a pastel pink or pale golden yellow room, add some spice with strong lime or jade-green touches. Tone down a rich orange, brown, or gold room with flashes of turquoise, mint green, or periwinkle blue. If the scheme is basically neutral, perhaps based on black, white, and gray, you can use strong, contrasting, warm accents—primary red, yellow, or orange—or cool ones—emerald green, vivid blue-violet, peacock blue.

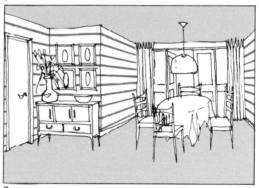

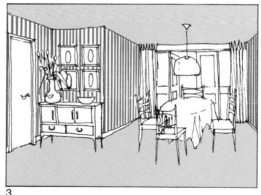

Color can be used to change the shape of a room as well as to create mood (right). Paint a high ceiling a dark, strong, rich, or bright color to make it seem lower. If it is very high, echo the color used on the floor (1). Horizontal stripes around a wall lower a high ceiling (2)—and vertical stripes make a room higher but smaller (3). To make a room seem less long, use a strong color on opposite walls (4).

Another way to build up a scheme is by using a favorite patterned fabric, floor covering, or wall covering that incorporates several colors for a starting point. Identify the component colors in the fabric and perhaps use the background color, particularly if it is neutral, for the ceiling and walls. Pick out a stronger color for furniture or bed covers and another for the windows. Choose a relatively bold or vibrant color for accents and accessories.

Creating a Mood

If you want to create a specific atmosphere or mood in a room, concentrate on colors that will create the desired impression and rely on furnishings and finishing touches to expand the effect. Each color has basic characteristics representing particular moods and associations, although of course response to color is individual.

Since tastes in color *are* individual, no person or trend should dictate what you choose,

A sunny impression is created in this space by the use of pale pink, apricot, and pastel yellow. Even the wood of the window bench, the floors, and the coffee table is light. Painting the room's spiring walls the same color as the couches makes the room seem more spacious. A profusion of color would crowd this room, so the accents are simple and delicate. The geometric green-and-pink pattern on the couch is echoed in throw pillows using similar colors in flowery patterns. Touches of blue and green provide contrast. To make the most of their graceful arch and the sunlight they let in, the windows are left unadorned.

COLOR MATCHING—THE PROFESSIONAL WAY

Color matching can never be a hit-or-miss affair. The only way to get it right is by color sampling: Take material or paper examples of existing items with you when you shop for the rest of the scheme. Add samples as you go along, take them all back home, and look at them in the actual environment in which they will be used, both in natural light and artificial light.

Make a color board from a piece of bristol board and use a large clip to hold the samples and design information. Start with your scale plan and proposed furniture positions and your list of measurements. Add samples of existing items or color-match to paint cards or chips. Build up the color scheme as you go along, adding new samples.

Do some sketches of the room, using colored overlays to outline the floor, wall, or furniture colors. This is a particularly good idea if you are undecided about your choices and if you like two or three different wall coverings, carpets, or fabrics. Make several color boards or sketches and seek a second opinion.

Try to obtain large samples of material or paper that has very strong color hues or is boldly patterned. A strong color or bold design will be even more dominant when seen over a large area. If possible, buy small sample cans of paints to test the color on an area of wall or piece of paper before making a decision.

but it is useful to know what is currently new and fresh so that you'll be aware of what is available in the stores and what array of colors you have to choose from.

The latest colors are highly saturated—brilliant tones without the graying or muting of previous years. So instead of murky green, for example, jungle green is now a favorite, and joyful pinks are replacing the mauves of

recent times. A wide range of neutrals is also available for using with these high-voltage colors, to balance them out. With the new awareness of the environment, a wide selection of fresh greens and blues is also showing up in paints and fabrics.

But no matter what the current color trends, the effects of basic colors remain the same:

Red Red is the color of vitality, energy, and aggressiveness. It is bright, exciting, and dramatic, but it can be overpowering and needs to be used with discretion. It is the strongest advancing color, making a room seem small, inviting, stimulating. It can make you feel physically warm; you could, for example, give a cold, clinical bathroom a warmer look with touches of red.

As red becomes less intense, it becomes softer and more delicate. Rose and pastel pinks are often used to create romantic bedrooms, but are considered perhaps too "sweet" for communal living areas and un-

In this simple bedroom, the furniture looks important because of the red bed cover and upholstery. In the second sketch the furniture fades into the background and the walls take over.

For some people a little red goes a long way, but for aficionados, red—the most strongly advancing color—is the most appealing. The owners of this candle-lit dining room obviously love red. The red walls have been painted with a ragging technique that gives the room dimensionality, and the table is covered with a red-patterned tablecloth. To cool this sizzling combination and to accentuate a china collection, the inside of the china cabinet is painted in a pale green shade similar to the one found in the tablecloth pattern.

businesslike for work areas. The deeper values of red, such as burgundy and plum tones, are rich and subtle. Their warmth and elegance can be used very effectively in traditional living rooms and large hallways.

Orange   Orange is very similar in character to red, and combines the physical energy of red with the intellectual associations of yellow. It is almost as dominant, intense, and advancing as red, and can be used in much the same way. It will create a highly stimulating scheme, particularly if it is contrasted with a neutral or complementary color. It is a good, lively color for children's rooms, playrooms, bathrooms, or any area where relaxation is not the main aim. When orange is lightened it becomes a peach or apricot tone and has a delicacy akin to that of the softer pinks. When orange is darkened to deep terra-cotta by adding tan or brown to it, it becomes a versatile earth color. These rich shades act as foils for either warm or cool colors and are effective when allowed to domi- nate a room that is slightly accented with cream or white. Unlike the restless, vivid hues of bright orange, these velvety orange-browns create a warm, relaxing atmosphere.

Yellow Yellow is a bright, joyful color, always reminiscent of sunshine. It is associated with the mind, intellect, creative energy, and power. Bright yellows are strong and stimulating, bringing warmth and light into cold dark rooms. But the stimulus of yellow can also be disruptive, so use it with care. It makes an ideal focal point but needs plenty

Lighten orange, and it becomes peach or apricot; darken it, and it becomes terra-cotta, tan, or brown. These are all very useful colors in a decorating scheme that relies on natural materials, such as wood or clay used in the pottery. Here the cool gray laminated tables are a textural and chromatic foil for the warm apricot shades used for the upholstery and curtains.

A bright, stimulating color, yellow is associated with creativity, energy, and new beginnings. Bright or pale yellow schemes can fill a room with sunshine. Gold, a darkened version of yellow, is an elegant color. When properly lit, it glows. In this sophisticated Southwestern dining room, the matte surface of the mustard walls makes a collection of gold and silver objects seem even more reflective. If you look closely, you can see the rest of the room reflected in one of the gold plates.

of neutral background to highlight it. Pale yellows are highly reflective and will make small, dark rooms seem larger and lighter. The darkened versions of yellow—mustard, gold, and golden brown—have a subdued glow that is rich, warm, and inviting. They are ideal for elegant, sophisticated schemes. When yellow tends toward green, such as golden olive, hues can look golden and interesting in daylight but appear dead, almost gray, in artificial light, so again, use with care.

Green Green is the color of nature. It is refreshing and easy on the eye because it is a balanced color falling between the naturally warm and cool ranges in the spectrum. Green tends to recede and creates an impression of space, particularly in its lighter values. It will bring a lush, vibrant atmosphere into a dull town house or a dim apartment. The darker, richer versions of green also help to bring a garden atmosphere inside, but, as in nature, all greens gain clarity from a few contrasting accents. Gray-green tones are also changed by artificial light.

Blue This is the color of harmony and peace, also associated with steadfastness and

Green is a versatile color that invites the best of nature indoors even on the coolest of winter days. On the spectrum, green falls between the warm and cool colors, so what you combine it with will alter its effect. Use green with blue and the effect is cooler, more subdued. In this sitting room, there's green in the stone surrounding the fireplace and green in the striped ticking of the couch and in the tapestry pillows. The rug is a green-blue reminiscent of tropical waters, and wooden fish stand poised as if to splash into it. The room is cool and spacious because green tends to recede, especially if it is pale.

Blue can be a demanding color, particularly when it's dark, and it benefits from contrasts. This kitchen's overall blue color scheme is balanced by snowy white woodwork and tiles and was probably inspired by the owners' collection of blue-and-white china. Blue-and-white checks and patterns on kitchen linens give the room a crisp and tidy look.

loyalty. It is basically a cool color, particularly in its paler tints when it creates an impression of wide vistas and skies. But blue can be very demanding in a pure, strong form, so use it with care in confined areas. It can also appear much colder than green, so warm it up, if necessary, with definite contrasts. Blue will diffuse and soften bright sunlight, since it is fairly low in reflectional value, so it will calm down a room that takes the full glare of the sun. The grayed versions of blue can be rather dull unless plenty of contrasting neutral and warm colors are used to set them off.

Violet Traditionally a powerful color—the imperial purple—violet in its strongest tones is vibrant and demanding, sometimes overpowering. Use with care, especially on a large scale, and add plenty of contrast in a room scheme. A purple or violet on the blue side of the spectrum can appear cold, so treat it as blue; red-violet is warm and has many of the characteristics of red. Pastel versions such as pale lilac or mauve can be either warm or cold and will be spacious or intimate, depending on the amount of blue or red in the basic color. Lilac is a romantic color, ideal for

Violet, lilac, and purple can be warm or cool, depending on the amount of blue (cool) or red (warm) in them. Stronger versions of these colors may be stimulating in small doses, but can be overpowering if they are not toned down by contrasts of white or gray. This living room uses several pale variations of violet, but tends toward the blue side of the spectrum, which makes is seem serene and spacious. The balance may change at dawn and dusk, when sunrises and sunsets warm the room's palette. Note the use of ceramic tile for the floor before the fireplace and leading to the lavender carpet. The fireplace has built-in storage space for firewood.

a bedroom. The deeper, grayed ''plummy'' tones of violet are rich, warm, and mysterious.

Once you have decided on the mood you want to create and the basic colors, make a separate color board for each room. If you are unsure about a scheme, or the decision is to be a shared one, you could prepare several alternative boards to consider different effects.

PATTERN AND TEXTURE

Pattern and textural contrast and variety can be used to heighten the mood and atmosphere created by color. A room composed entirely of plain surfaces may lack interest, however good the color scheme. The balance between pattern and surface texture in a room must be as carefully and skillfully selected as the color scheme. Patterns and textures set the style of the room, whether it be modern or traditional, or planned to evoke a specific period flavor.

Scale is an all-important element in the choice of patterns. The design should in each case relate to the size of the area in which it will be used. Nothing looks worse than wallpaper with an enormous pattern crammed onto small or heavily recessed walls, or on walls peppered with tiny windows. This is especially true if the design has recognizable motifs—birds, flowers, trees, or figures—that may be cut off at awkward points. The same principle should be applied to upholstery and pillows. When covering a chair, for example, choose a pattern that successfully fills the shape of the chair back, seat, or cushion. A bold pattern covering a small area of floor can make your every step uncertain; it may play optical tricks that are particularly unwelcome on a surface that should be seen as completely stable. Conversely, very small,

COLOR—IDEAS AND GUIDELINES

When you have studied the theory of color and understand the basic relationships of colors, you can apply certain rules—or break them with reasonable knowledge of the likely effect. The following guidelines may be helpful:

- Always relate the color scheme to the actual room—consider its size, shape, and intrinsic mood.
- Use color to help create mood and atmosphere—warm colors for an intimate, cozy effect and cool hues for a more spacious, elegant feel.
- Decorate ''cold'' rooms mainly in warm colors such as red, orange, and yellow, and ''warm'' rooms in cool colors such as blue, green, and gray.
- Introduce some sharp color contrasts or accents to emphasize a scheme—light against dark, pure hues against paler tones, warm colors against cool ones.
- Decorate large rooms in stronger, richer, or darker colors and bold patterns.
- Use light, cool colors to make a small room seem more spacious. Feature small-scale patterns that won't dominate the space.
- Use bright, advancing, or contrasting colors to create a stimulating, active environment. Use pale, receding, or neutral colors, or a monochromatic scheme, to suggest a relaxing atmosphere.
- Consider the value of neutral colors as a link between pure hues or to tone down a strong, dominating color scheme.

discreet patterns can make no impact at all if used over a large floor area.

Pattern tends to behave in the same way as color does. Bolder designs come toward you and make the surface on which they are used look smaller. Simpler designs seem to recede,

Varying intense patterns can wage a visual war or they can make a room bright and lively. In this room, a variety of bright patterns happily coexists against an unconventional background. It works because the patterns share similar colors—reds, oranges, blacks, and beigy whites—and the room's black walls and white fittings and trim need strong colors to enliven them. In contrast to the rough weave of the blankets and rough surfaces of the primitive decorations, lacy blinds hang from the skylights within the beamed ceilings.

creating an impression of more space. A boldly patterned surface often appears to be even more dominant than a strong, solid color, particularly if it is multicolored and includes strong, clear hues. A pale, patterned surface will usually be slightly more vibrant than a light, solid color, but this depends upon the scale and color balance of the pattern.

Patterns fall into many different categories, and within each division there is a good deal of variety. The following are the basic styles used in decorating materials:

Florals These can be neat and pretty, country-house chintzy, small and sprightly, full-blown or neatly regimented. Any of these styles may also be combined with stripes or other more formal patterning.

Geometrics   Geometrics range from classical architectural forms to vibrantly contemporary, unconventional arrangements.

Abstracts   Abstract patterns sometimes suggest simple forms and shapes, but more often they make use of artistic techniques—such as the stippled surface of pointillism; the soft, blurred look of watercolor; or the scribbled effect of crayon drawing—to create a look, rather than a specific picture.

Checks and stripes   These patterns perform the same function as neutral colors, acting as a break or link in a scheme, possibly bridging the gap between two different designs, or between patterned and plain surfaces.

Traditional designs   Of various types, these derive from existing and accepted styles such as Classical, Georgian, Regency, Victorian, Edwardian, Art Nouveau, Art Deco, and 1950s.

Ethnic patterns   Cultural influences form these styles: African, Oriental, Asian, Indian, Mexican, and Hawaiian.

Picturesque patterns   Highly representational, these patterns simulate scenes or characters. Many are designed for specific age groups, such as small children or teenagers.

Graphic or stylized patterns   These can also be highly representational, but are often abstract. Some are specially designed to simulate computer graphics.

PATTERN—IDEAS AND GUIDELINES

- Mix two of a kind—florals with florals, geometrics with geometrics. When mixing different types of pattern, create links between colors and basic shapes.
- Use simple checks or stripes as a link or contrast.
- Pay attention to scale—feature large patterns for big walls, floors, and windows, and tiny patterns on small surfaces.
- Mix patterned surfaces with solids to give high contrast and visual impact.
- Strong designs tend to come forward and make a room look smaller. Small or subtle patterns fade away and make a room appear larger.
- Choose the right type of design to suit the room style or to enhance furnishings. When choosing contrasts, always try to see a large sample of patterned surfaces. Make sure they are stimulating, not overwhelming.
- Put several solid-colored items together, using the colors to create a patterned effect.
- Introduce patterned accessories into a room where too many plain surfaces have created a dull appearance.

Coordinated materials in all of the styles described above are widely available in a range of different surface materials and products. Some lines offer total coordination throughout the home, including curtains and upholstery, fabrics and trims, wall coverings and borders, bed linens, floor coverings, and bathroom and kitchen accessories. Coordinating does not necessarily mean "matching"—in fact, "mixing together" would be a better description. The patterns can be on a different scale but coordinated by shape and color, for example, or have the same scale and colors but in different designs, such as florals and stripes. Wall coverings and fabrics may have two, three, or four distinct but co-ordinating designs, with one border or recurring pattern unifying them. It is not unusual to see many patterns layered or used very close to one another, say one for upholstery, one for curtains, one for wallpaper, and another for a tablecloth or bedspread, and they all complement and enhance one another, creating a complete, finished, and definitely designed look.

A fully coordinated range can make a room appear surprisingly grand and spacious yet inviting and comfortable, as long as the patterns are not very large or very brightly colored. Keeping the floor, be it wall-to-wall carpeting or plain hardwood, one color and without pattern also prevents the overall de-

sign and the room itself from looking busy or overwhelming.

Making Your Own Match

How can you successfully mix interesting patterns and textures in a room? The secret is to mix like with like, selecting patterns and colors that relate to one another in some way. You may find this will mean selecting merchandise from the same manufacturer—most wall covering, fabric, and flooring manufacturers work to a specific color palette, certainly within each season, so many different designs will appear in the same colors or relate to a basic color range.

Mixing like with like means matching some common elements of the patterns—putting two or three floral prints together, keeping a theme or particular color range, or

Patterns can work together successfully, even if they are not part of a coordinated collection. The secret is to mix like with like, or use a "neutral" pattern such as a check, trellis, or stripe to link together two designs, or coordinate a pattern and a plain. Geometric patterns can be modern and graphic or classical and architectural (top left). Traditional paisley, classic stripe, and basketweave effect work well with a subtle pearlized plain (top right). Abstracts and simulations work well together (bottom left). Stripes, diamond trellis, and chevron designs look good together against a marbled background. (bottom right)

using similar shapes of different sizes but the same basic proportions. Simple stripes, checks, weaves, trellis effects, and heavily textured solids can act as links between two other patterns or may help to tone down a heavily patterned color scheme. They can also be used very effectively on their own to give life to a very plain room. Using the same pattern, or a very similar one, in varying sizes can work well, following the basic rule of relating the scale of the pattern to the scale of the surface on which it will be seen.

Imagining how a pattern will look in a large space can be difficult if you only have a small sample. It is often surprising to see how a pattern changes over a broad area. A roll of wallpaper or a bolt of fabric has its own appearance when first seen by itself, but it looks very different when actually covering something. If you are planning to use a strong pattern, look at two rolls of wall covering placed side by side with edges aligned, or look at two whole widths and the full drop of the fabric proposed for curtains. Curtain fabrics will always be seen gathered or pleated, never perfectly flat, which will alter the appearance of the pattern. Gather up a handful of fabric to get an idea of how it will look when it has been transformed into the purpose you have in mind.

Items such as ceramic wall and floor tiles can be equally deceptive. Select these from a store where you can see mounted display boards of the same design of wall tiles, and where floor tiles can be placed in mirrored boxes, which magnify a square section of tiling almost to room size. If you cannot see the actual items enhanced this way, there are catalogs and brochures with photographs designed to show an overall impression of the effect, although they are not necessarily accurate for color matching.

Carpets and other floor coverings are sometimes hard to judge, especially if you are choosing a narrow width. Try to view as large a piece as possible on the floor, ideally with two pieces side by side. Again, pictures in brochures and catalogs can show you a more realistic effect and may help you reach a decision.

Patterning with Solids

The simplest example of this concept is the way in which several different colors of plain floor tiles can be laid in a pattern—for example, stripes, diamonds, or a checkerboard effect—or to outline specific objects. Plain wall tiles can be used in the same way. Two or three different-colored plain fabrics can be sewn together into curtains or made into a patchwork quilt, creating patterning by simple means. Objects and accessories can be cleverly arranged—for example, colored cushions on a bed, sofa, or chair, or a variety of houseplants grouped together.

Another way of patterning is by using special painting techniques, such as dragging, rag rolling, or sponge stippling, on walls and woodwork. The effects of some paint techniques are so subtle that they barely qualify as patterning, but they nevertheless create a more interesting surface texture than a completely flat coat of paint and contribute to a feeling of space, particularly in a small room.

Textural Emphasis

Just as certain patterns create a sense of style, so do certain textures. Some are frankly homespun, some are opulent, and others can be starkly rough. Canvas, leather, chrome, and loosely woven or open-weave fabrics suit a contemporary setting, while brass, velvet, and satin may be more appropriate to a traditional style. Ceramics and pottery, glass,

These traditional painting techniques give an interesting texture to walls and woodwork—almost a raised or dimensional quality.

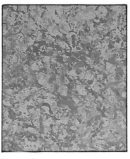
Sponging

Dragging

Ragging

Rag rolling

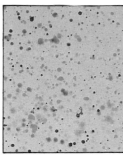
Spattering

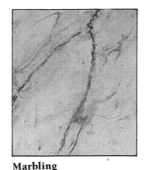
Marbling

Marbling with jointing

Wood graining

TEXTURE—IDEAS AND GUIDELINES

- Use different textures to emphasize a design and to contrast with each other.
- Select surface textures that suit the overall furnishing and decorating style.
- Make use of shiny or reflective surfaces to increase the apparent size of a small room. Work with matte, soft textures to make a large room seem smaller and more intimate.
- Use a heavily textured material to hide a poor, uneven surface.
- In a monochromatic scheme, make use of contrasting textures to enliven areas of solid color.
- Exploit the textural values of translucent or coarsely woven fabrics, allowing them to filter the natural or artificial light into a room, either gently or more vibrantly.

brick, slate, and wood will fit into many different styles.

Texture is linked inextricably with color and light. Some surfaces absorb light, while others bounce it back at you, and these properties can make a color appear quite different, even if the same dye or pigment has been used. Shiny textures, such as gloss paint, mirrors, highly polished surfaces, and glass, all reflect light to such an extent that they will increase the apparent size of the room. Very dull, matte textures such as nubby-textured carpets, tweed upholstery, and velvet have the opposite effect. They also help to absorb sound. Other textures, such as lace and open-weave fabrics, rattan and cane furniture, wrought-iron tracery, and trellised screens, have qualities that allow the light to filter delicately through the material, rather than be absorbed or bounced back.

Take into account the quality of the surface before choosing a textured covering. Gloss paint, silks, and satins all show up any imperfections in a surface. Heavily textured, matte fabrics, wall coverings, and floorings conceal uneven, dented, or scratched surfaces, and thickly textured paints cover up surface damage on walls and ceilings.

DESIGN IN PRACTICE

PUTTING THE DESIGN PRINCIPLES OUTLINED IN
Section One into practice involves getting down to specifics. In the following
pages, "Room-by-Room Design" takes you through each room or area of your house
or apartment and illustrates in detail the stages of planning and design that will enable
you to bring about the distinctive style and atmosphere you have chosen. For each
room there are suggested approaches to the design, and pointers on style, color,
surface treatments, and lighting. The approach you choose will depend on several
factors, including the space available and the main function of the room.

Whether you are planning an entire renovation or just minor alterations, it is
essential to consider the room as a complete entity. You must take into account style,
atmosphere, and function, together with existing decoration, architectural features
including windows, and any furnishings you may already have. The initial step of
deciding on a scheme can sometimes seem the most difficult to take, so looking at
other people's interior design ideas can be a useful and time-saving exercise. The wide
range of styles illustrated in Section Four of this book also may help you come to a
decision. Interior design and home-improvement magazines are other rich sources of
information.

"Tricks of the Light" emphasizes the importance of planning lighting at the initial
stage of any new design and illustrates in detail how to achieve different lighting
effects.

"Ways with Windows" is a comprehensive guide to window treatments for all
shapes, sizes, and styles of windows. Several alternative treatments are suggested for
each window type so that you can select a style to blend in with your overall room
design.

Room-by-Room Design

No two households have the same life-style or living requirements, and when you take over a new house or apartment you may find problems that need immediate solutions. Assess each room or area individually, rather than tackling everything at once.

The best way to approach a difficult room is by making a list of its good features, faults, and drawbacks, and if necessary taking its dimensions and making a room plan to scale (see page 10 12). This is the time to call in expert help for advice and estimates on any structural alterations.

If the area that needs changing is the bathroom or kitchen, you may well have to start by collecting literature on available equipment and appliances before you ask a kitchen planner, plumber, or electrician in to discuss the necessary work. It always helps to have an idea of exactly what you want when rethinking any room, but it is equally important to be flexible and to listen to the constructive suggestions of the experts. If the house seems to have several tricky structural problems, it is sensible to call in an architect or builder right at the initial planning stage. But they don't have to live with the end result; you need to know what *you* want to be able to brief them properly. If you don't like the plans and suggestions submitted by a professional, don't be afraid to say so. Ask for a perspective drawing if you cannot visualize the plan and try to work with the expert to achieve the right solution.

Shortage of space or the best utilization of space is a major concern in many homes. It may well be feasible to convert or extend the property, but it may be wiser to look at the house as a whole, and to rethink and replan the purpose and function of some of the rooms. Bedrooms do not always have to be upstairs, and living rooms do not always have to be downstairs. A downstairs room opening to the outside can make an ideal playroom/bedroom for two or more children. It may be possible to install a second bathroom or convert part of a bedroom to one to ease the morning rush. A garage that is not used much could be converted into a laundry, den, or playroom.

Coming to grips with design problems comes down to tailoring your home to suit you and your family's requirements, and then decorating and furnishing each room to give the greatest enjoyment to those who use them.

Entryways and Foyers

A visitor's first impression of a home starts at the front door. If you have an older home, it may already have a very attractive front door that might just need a face lift. Sometimes an interesting front door can be vastly improved with fresh paint and new hardware—stylish handles, knobs, a knocker, and a letter slot—or with a different style of numbering or lettering.

The entry hall or foyer provides an introduction to the interior decoration of the house and should have its own impact. It can be slightly more theatrical in style than other areas in the home; even a small, cramped hall can be treated dramatically. This may be an opportunity to use bold, unusual colors such as pumpkin, dark eggplant, or bright pink. In some cases, however, the hall, stairs, and landing will need to bring together the different color schemes and designs used in various rooms throughout the house to create a feeling of harmony and continuity from area to area.

Because halls are sometimes difficult to decorate, they may be redesigned less frequently than other rooms, or they may be neglected, being lined with a bland patterned wallpaper or painted a neutral color. A hall, however, should be designed with the same care, skill, and flair as the main living areas. It needs the same considerations of style, atmosphere, size, and shape. Above all, the aim is to create an attractive, welcoming impression.

Because entryways usually contain little furniture, most halls do not need the substantive planning required for other rooms; however, if they are examined within the context of whole-house planning, it may be possible to utilize the space and make the hall a dual-purpose area. Space under the stairs can often be opened out to make a small home office or hobby area, or simply to form an alcove where an attractive piece of furniture can be displayed and dramatically lit. The alcove could also be filled with lighted display shelves or used as a well-organized storage area. Or it might contain a small bookcase,

chair, and lamp to create a miniature library or reading "room."

If the hall is very small, you may be able to play some visual tricks to make it seem larger with mirrors and a light color scheme. The space will need to be carefully and practically planned, however, to accommodate such objects as hat racks; coat pegs; a shelf for keys, mail, and gloves; and possibly a telephone table or narrow storage chest.

One way of creating more space is to take down a wall or part of one between a very narrow hall and the downstairs rooms. Think very carefully before you do this, however. Do you really want to walk straight into the living room from the street? Then, too, interior walls between halls and living rooms are frequently load-bearing, and a builder will probably have to be called in to survey the situation and to make the change.

THE LOOK

Making an entrance hall work well may involve solving several design problems. Hall, stair, and landing areas often suffer from being awkwardly shaped, for example. An inviting, spacious-looking entrance hall or foyer, with a well-coordinated color scheme and attractive flooring, is the ideal to aim for.

Style

The hall should have its own distinctive style, while at the same time giving a glimpse of the design features to come in other rooms. It should also blend in with the architectural character of the home and be considered in relation to the exterior of the building.

If the hall is entered from a dreary corridor or boxy elevator, or directly off a busy street, it can serve to relieve the effect of these environments by creating an immediate im-

An entrance can be dramatic or modestly appealing—it's a matter of personal style. Whatever you choose, the first glimpse of your home should be welcoming. This glittering drama of a doorway only took a little paint, applied in a technique called **sponging,** to make it unique. Twin columns standing before a gilded wall add to the drama and are fitted with a security camera. Asymmetrical moldings provide another cosmetic change that adds visual interest without making structural changes.

This hallway uses simple elements to define its Colonial style and invite exploration. The pleasingly symmetrical turn of the stairs and octagonal landing window are balanced by the rectangular Colonial jelly cupboard, which can serve as a perfect storage place for gloves and hats. The front door is painted a similar shade to the cupboard's blue-green and to the blue woven into the geometrically patterned rug. Wooden decoy ducks, baskets, and an American flag quilt also define style, and a glimpse of a hanging textile lures you up the stairs for a closer look.

pression of comfort and a welcoming atmosphere—perhaps by containing many well-cared-for plants or just by creating a feeling of warmth with contemporary or period paint, wallpaper, fabric, and accessories.

If, on the other hand, the exterior of the home is pleasing, do your best to match the interior with the exterior. If the house and the neighborhood have a particular style, echo it on the inside right at the entryway. Let the basic character of the house take over. A country style, for example, works well in a country house, with quarry tiles for the floor, arrangements of dried grasses, woven or wicker baskets, and colorful flower displays. In a city apartment or town house, go for a more sophisticated look, perhaps with one or two elegant chairs and a series of prints. Another way to make a smooth transition from the exterior to the interior is to use a paint color for the entryway that is similar to the color used on the outside of the house or the corridor of the apartment building.

Color

Colors can be chosen to create the look of spaciousness often needed in an entryway and to give a cozy feel or a cool, elegant quality. Whether you opt for a more dramatic rich, dark, bright, or layered scheme, or for a pale, restrained one, use colors that to some degree link visually with the rooms leading off the entryway to unify the space. This produces a more streamlined effect and, in a small house, gives a feeling of greater space.

Areas of interest can be created with well-chosen furniture and accessories, particularly if they are unusual or witty. Don't forget to have fun: Lacquer the walls in dark jewel tones with a mirror added for sparkle, place elegant vases prominently, or use "found objects," such as weather vanes, as sculptural

focal points. A plant stand filled with blooms also introduces a touch of natural color.

Some halls can be used very effectively to display pictures. For example, you can feature an assortment of colorful paintings and prints on one wall. The colors can echo those used in other rooms as an additional means of achieving color continuity, if that is a priority. Other accessories can similarly be used as links. But be aware of how adjacent floor coverings look in relation to one another.

Surfaces

These should be practical, particularly in a house or apartment where all traffic has to go through the hall. Most important, floor coverings should be of good quality and hardwearing. A washable floor is the most useful surface, especially for a busy family comprised of several small children and pets. Ceramic tiles, linoleum, or vinyl floors are all ideal. If you prefer to use rugs in the entryway, a patterned rug will conceal dirt, and a colorful sisal carpet that can easily be replaced when dirty is an inexpensive solution.

Stairs are probably best carpeted since the material prevents slipping, but if you do want to show the exposed wood, seal—instead of polishing—the steps with a matte nonslip sealer. Floorboards, stripped and decorated with stain, paint, or stencils, or with one of the special painting techniques, make a practical, decorative alternative to carpet.

Woodwork, particularly baseboards and doors, are subject to a lot of wear in the hall so a strong color is worth considering as an alternative to white or a pale neutral. Stripping the wood back to the bare essentials and sealing or polishing it will provide an easy-care surface. Walls at the side of stairs should be washable.

Lighting

Lighting needs to be fairly bright in the hall, stair, and landing areas. Light the front porch or door area and control it with switches positioned inside and out. Light the hall or telephone table, mirror, and hall closet with good direct lighting, such as wall sconces, spots, or lamps. Also light the stair-case so that the treads and risers are clearly defined. This may require several light fixtures. Always have switches for these areas both downstairs and upstairs. In very large houses, arrange the wiring so that all the lights can be switched on or off from the ground floor, and then from level to level.

Kitchens

The kitchen is one of the most frequently used rooms in a home, but is often the most poorly designed. It may simply be that the appearance of your kitchen is not right—a situation that can be changed with new color schemes, accessories, and possibly a new selection of appliances. But your kitchen may also be unsuitable for your requirements. Do not rush to rip out all the existing cupboards, appliances, and sinks, however. Sometimes it pays to live with mistakes until you are quite sure of your real needs, and until you decide exactly what ought to be replaced and what can be retained. Over the years you will also find that your needs change with altered living patterns.

Kitchen manufacturers' brochures are not usually much help when it comes to designing a functional room and figuring out how to fit everything you want into the space available. A pretty picture may help to stimulate ideas for style and color schemes, but a kitchen in particular must be planned from a practical and functional point of view. To be able to work out just what you want *before* you can brief a builder or professional planner, you need to understand the basic principles of kitchen design.

HOW TO PLAN A KITCHEN

Since safety, efficiency, and economy of movement are crucial in a kitchen, you must plan out a sensible "work triangle" within the available space. The shape of the kitchen obviously will influence where and how you do this. Common kitchen layouts include the single line, the galley, the L-shape, the U-shape, and the island. The basic shape of your kitchen and its individual requirements may involve variations on these themes.

The general aim, however, is to reduce the amount of walking between food storage, food preparation, and cooking areas—that is, between the refrigerator, sink, work surfaces, and stove. The ideal kitchen work triangle should have sides of not less than 11¾ feet and not more than 21½ feet.

The location of appliances is important. Try not to place the stove opposite the sink because of the danger of accidents when moving across the room with hot pans. Similarly, a door should never cross the route from the stove to the sink. A refrigerator or freezer is best positioned away from the stove, even if they are well insulated, and there should be adequate work surfaces on

All too often style in a kitchen is obscured by the practicalities of fitting in the necessary equipment and deciding on the appliances. Although it's the scrubbed pine, the baskets, the topiary, the cherry-colored cabinets, chairs, and patterned china that make this kitchen milk-and-cookies cozy, it's the efficient layout that makes it a pleasure in which to work. The floor plan spaces furniture and appliances so that there's a minimum of walking while cooking or cleaning up. Skylights illuminate tasks in an otherwise windowless work space.

both sides of the stove. Group tall units such as storage cupboards together, preferably at the end of a run of units. Never put a wall cupboard alone on a blank area of wall; try to position an appliance or the sink underneath it. Do not, however, put wall cupboards above or too close to cooking areas, since grease tends to drift up from them.

Aim to zone the areas—utility, eating, and working. The utility area may include storage cupboards for mops, brooms, ironing boards, and cleaning materials, and possibly laundry appliances such as a washer and dryer. Ideally, however, the laundry area should be in a separate room, such as a converted storeroom or a second-floor space that is conveniently close to bedrooms and bathrooms.

Every kitchen needs an eating area, however small—a pull-out work surface and stool can be enough for a small meal. A good arrangement is a separate dining section with an extending table, divided from the rest of the kitchen.

The working area is where you position the

THE KITCHEN WORK TRIANGLE

F-shaped

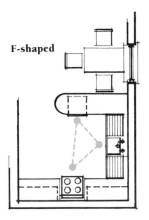

A fairly large kitchen can be divided into kitchen and dining areas, separated by a breakfast bar. Extra storage can be provided in ceiling-mounted cabinets above. The work triangle fits neatly into the cooking and food preparation area. The serving area is positioned near the table in this practical layout.

U-shaped

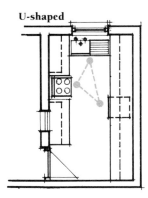

Long, narrow kitchens can have units, work surfaces, and appliances fitted around three sides, if there is only one door to the room. The work triangle should be kept as tight as possible. Don't position the stove opposite the sink because of potential accidents with hot pans.

L-shaped

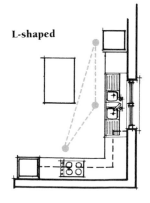

A large, square kitchen can have units and appliances around two sides, with a large multipurpose table in the center. Avoid the temptation to extend the triangle too far—the distance between sink, food storage and preparation, and stove should be kept under 20 feet.

work triangle. It consists of a food storage and preparation area, and a place for cooking, serving, dishwashing, and storage of dinnerware. To be realistic, the areas will overlap to some extent in most situations, and many of the surfaces will be dual-purpose.

As well as fitting everything into the room, you will need to think three-dimensionally and make sure the units and work surfaces are comfortable to use. Position wall cupboards high enough above worktops so that you don't bump your head, but not so high that you can't reach things. Allow for units to fit under windowsills, and place appliances such as the dishwasher, refrigerator, or freezer under work surfaces, or alternatively stacked on top of one another.

Think carefully about the interior planning of units and cupboards. There are many types of interior storage fittings, such as pull-out sliding racks and baskets, carousel sections, and circular revolving shelves, which help to keep everything clean, neat, and easy to reach. You can also adapt other storage items for the interiors of kitchen cupboards and units—some office equipment, such as filing or letter trays, can be very useful in the kitchen for storing small objects or utensils. You may also be able to use the back of a door for hanging some small items, but be careful not to overload or the door may sag on its hinges.

Always consider lighting and electrical outlets at the initial planning stage and plan for more than enough outlets—you will always need double the number you thought were sufficient. Alternatively, you could use a series of track systems that have outlets along their length. Build in flexibility so that small appliances can be moved and plugged in at will. Light all surfaces well—sink, stove, and food preparation and dining areas in partic-

---

KITCHEN SAFETY

When planning or installing a kitchen, carefully consider the following safety aspects:

1. Keep a small fire extinguisher handy for dousing burning fat or possible flare-ups from burners.
2. Position small appliances out of reach of young children.
3. Keep electrical wires and plugs well away from the water supply.
4. Include more than enough electrical outlets in your kitchen plan to avoid overloading adapter units.

---

ular—and remember that although the sink may be under the window and well lit during the daylight hours, it also needs lighting at night. Have the various zones separately lit and controlled, so that you can darken the working part of the room if you want to create an intimate atmosphere for dining.

Adequate ventilation is very important and needs to be thought about early on in relation to the position of the units and appliances—installation of ducts for air-conditioning or the running of electrical wires through walls is semistructural and should be done at the start. Stoves can be fitted with unvented hoods that recirculate the air, removing odors but not humidity. A hood with a vent fitted to the outside will remove odors, humidity, and a certain amount of heat. Fans set into the windows or outside wall remove the steamy vapors that cause condensation. Place a fan as high up as possible and as near to the stove as you can. The correct size for your kitchen will be one that circulates the air 10 to 15 times per hour.

Following these basic principles of planning, you should be able to list your present

Always consider lighting and electrical outlets when planning a kitchen. There are never enough outlets unless they're given serious advance consideration. Light all surfaces well—the sink, the oven, and the food-preparation and dining areas. Ideally, as in this contemporary kitchen, the areas should be separately lit and controlled so that you can dim the lights in the work triangle while enjoying an intimate dinner.

and future requirements, leaving room for additions at a later stage. There is, of course, more to creating a kitchen than devising a workable plan. As with every other room, you will want to achieve a certain ambience and style, improve on any basic design faults, and enhance the positive features. If the room is basically well planned and attractive, you may only need to do a face-lift operation by redecorating, tiling, or perhaps adding new unit doors, to bring it up to your standards. If you decide you just do not have enough space, you may have to consider extending outward or converting inward, but again professional advice should be sought for any alteration as major as this.

Installation Once you know what you want, decide how to get the kitchen installed. This can be done in several different ways. You can buy self-assembly units and basic appliances and install and decorate them yourself or with the help of a carpenter. You can go to a builder, plan the kitchen together, and supervise the installation. Cabinets and other units may even be custom-built to your requirements. Alternatively, there are specialists who can provide total design services. Try interior design or architectural firms, specialty kitchen shops, or the kitchen section of department stores. Specialists may quote for assembly-on-site, assembled, or custom-built units, depending on your requirements. Some professional installers will not undertake structural alterations, so you may need the services of a builder, electrician, and plumber as well; any final decoration will probably be up to you.

THE LOOK

Apart from being well planned and well equipped, your kitchen should express your

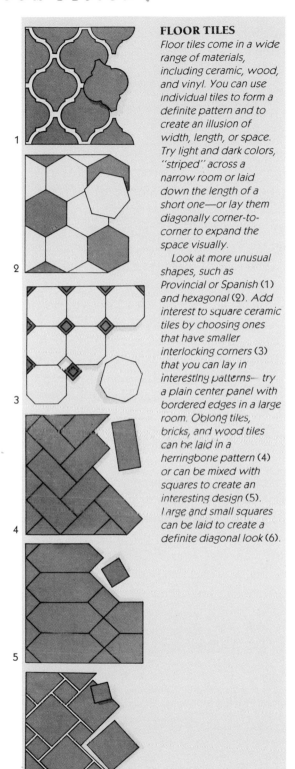

FLOOR TILES

Floor tiles come in a wide range of materials, including ceramic, wood, and vinyl. You can use individual tiles to form a definite pattern and to create an illusion of width, length, or space. Try light and dark colors, "striped" across a narrow room or laid down the length of a short one—or lay them diagonally corner-to-corner to expand the space visually.

Look at more unusual shapes, such as Provincial or Spanish (1) and hexagonal (2). Add interest to square ceramic tiles by choosing ones that have smaller interlocking corners (3) that you can lay in interesting patterns— try a plain center panel with bordered edges in a large room. Oblong tiles, bricks, and wood tiles can be laid in a herringbone pattern (4) or can be mixed with squares to create an interesting design (5). Large and small squares can be laid to create a definite diagonal look (6).

style and have some atmosphere as well. But in the kitchen, esthetic and practical considerations must go hand in hand. You have to combine your stylistic ideas for an attractive kitchen with a plan that is workable.

Style   Design the kitchen to suit yourself. The style can be country, English or French traditional, French provincial, Spanish, streamlined Scandinavian, high tech, American Southwest. There are as many possibilities as there are ways of cooking. You will need to select a style to suit the size and shape of the room, though. For example, a country farmhouse kitchen with stripped-pine dressers and a large scrubbed-pine table in the center will just not work in a small room (for ideas see ''A Sense of Style,'' pages 133–39). You will need to choose units that are in keeping with the basic look—natural wood for the farmhouse, streamlined, bright units for modern.

Color   Color can be used to create the basic atmosphere. As most kitchens tend to be fairly hot and steamy, cool color schemes work well. Basic color planning rules apply just as much to kitchens as to other rooms in the house, so use paler colors and restrained patterns in a small room (see pages 128–29), but try some unusual colors, like a pretty pastel pink or cool, elegant gray. Accent colors can be extremely striking in accessories.

Alternative kitchen lighting schemes are shown here. Fluorescent lighting beneath wall and ceiling-mounted units (1). Individual spot and fluorescent lighting positioned over work surfaces (2). Overhead lighting from a fluorescent fixture combined with bright concealed lighting above stove and surrounding work surfaces (3). Concealed lighting beneath run of units with the option of softer lighting over the table (4).

1

2

3

4

Surfaces   In the kitchen, particularly, working surfaces need to be practical. Although quarry tiles and flagstones create an authentic look on a country kitchen floor, they are hard on the feet and fatal to dropped dishes. They can be combined with strategically placed informal rugs or mats to counteract these problems, however. Quarry tiles are available in a variety of earth colors, including terra-cotta and mottled heather, in a variety of sizes and shapes. Cushioned vinyls are warmer, easy to clean, and bouncy underfoot. In large kitchens the dining area can have a carpet as a softer floor covering. Hardwood floors are an excellent surface for a kitchen floor but need a polyurethane coating. Work surfaces can be tiled or covered with plastic laminate, wood, or metal, depending on the unit type and the room style. But choose a work surface that is not too shiny, brightly colored, or jazzy, otherwise it will soon become tiring on the eyes.

Walls can be finished in any number of ways, from wood paneling to paint or washable wallpaper. A matte finish for paint is more practical than gloss because a high shine attracts condensation. Similarly, ceramic tiles are not practical for all the walls if the kitchen tends to steam up, but they make ideal splashbacks and focal points for the sink, work surfaces, and the stove.

Window treatments should be simple and easy to clean, particularly for windows near the cooking area. Pull-down shades are ideal and can easily be coordinated with wall treatments or used to create a splash of color. Curtains will need to be washed fairly often, so the fabric should be colorfast. Venetian blinds are time-consuming to clean, and are best kept away from the cooking area.

Lighting   Kitchen lighting requires careful consideration at the planning stage. Light all the work surfaces, the sink, and the stove with good direct lighting. Fit any deep cupboards with a light, positioning the light switch on the doorjamb so that the light comes on automatically when the door is opened. Light the table with direct but non-dazzling light—for example, with a shaded lamp or suspended candelabra or white globe light. In a large kitchen, install some subdued background lighting or put the direct light on a dimmer switch.

Bathrooms

The bathroom is similar to the kitchen in many ways and may share some of the same problems: lack of space, lack of storage, and outdated equipment.

Replanning a bathroom has to be done just as carefully and precisely as a kitchen, in order to place the components in the best possible positions and to make any alterations to the plumbing relatively easy. As with the kitchen, even if you plan to call in the experts, it helps to work out beforehand exactly what you want.

Above all, a bathroom should be planned for comfort. It should be warm in winter and cool in summer, and be functional without lacking personality. Everything should be positioned with practicality in mind—people need to be able to get in and out of the shower with ease and kneel down beside a bath when bathing small children and cleaning the tub.

The sink and toilet should be at the right levels. Towels should be easy to reach. There are certain recommended measurements and distances to follow as a guide.

BATHROOM PLANNING

Large and even small bathrooms can have whirlpool massage baths, shower massages, saunas, Jacuzzis, and steam baths. Bathtubs come in a range of exotic shapes—circular, sculpturally shaped, or designed to fit into a corner. Before you decide to purchase one of these tubs, check with a plumber to make sure your boiler and hot water heater are large enough to cope with the increased demands for hot water. Also ask your builder to check and ensure that the floor can sustain the extra weight of these fixtures.

If you have to install several new items, start with an accurate scale plan. Draw in the existing items and superimpose the new ones. Such a plan will show how much of the plumbing needs to be changed, and how much room you have for improvement.

Bathroom fixtures include a bathtub, an integral or separate shower, a single or double sink, a toilet, and perhaps a bidet. You may want to put a shower in the guest bathroom so that you have an extra facility to ease the morning rush.

Collect bathroom equipment catalogs and look at the type of fixtures available. Once you have some idea of the color and style of the equipment you would like to install, make a formal bathroom plan. Many manufacturers' brochures include graph paper for making plans and even supply bathtub and sink shapes to the same scale, so that you can move the shapes around on the room plan to determine the best position for each.

As with a kitchen, you need to think three-

When planning the bathroom, it is essential to plan for people! It is no good fitting in all the equipment and then finding everything is too close together to be used comfortably. There are certain suggested minimum measurements for user space of various items—you need to be able to step in and out of the shower stall or bath, for example.

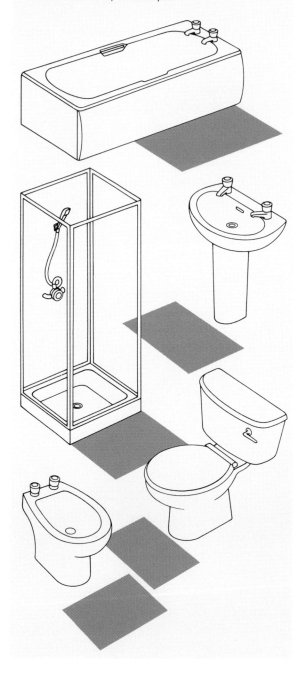

BATHROOM FIXTURES

Fixtures should be functional but have style. Choose ones to suit both your bathroom and your budget. Try to plan ahead and think what your requirements are likely to be in two or three years' time—bathrooms should not need new fixtures too often.

Sinks come in all shapes and sizes, with or without pedestals. Choose a comfortable height for the majority of users in the family, and look for ease of cleaning and style.

Toilets should be comfortable and at the correct height for the users.

Bathtubs are now part of the technological revolution, but decide on shape and size before thinking about spa or whirlpool extras. Showers can be on their own or over the bath. Bidets should be at the correct height for the users.

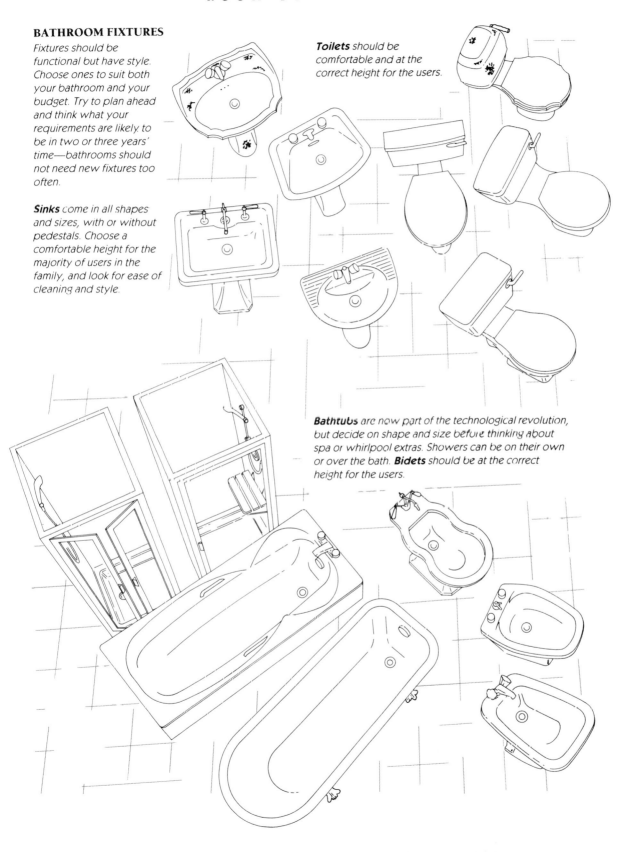

Bathrooms can be as pretty and as personal as any other room in the house. Once the practical planning aspects have been considered and the plumbing is in, the finishing touches are up to you. A warm color scheme gives this bathroom's white tiles and fixtures a rosy glow. Pink-striped wallpaper and window swags soften the room's clean, simple lines, while marble floor tiles add visual interest. A wooden chest provides storage space for extra bath linens, toys, or toiletries.

dimensionally to make sure that sinks, toilets, and bidets will fit under windows. Also allow enough space vertically to accommodate a shower stall, if desired. Plan in conjunction with recommended measurements or distances.

Once you have an idea of what you want and where to put it, you can call in the plumber, contractor, or bathroom specialist. Obtain several different estimates for the work involved, and check the company's or individual's credentials with the National

Across the room, the cabinets under the sinks provide more storage space. The porcelain sinks are patterned in pink flowers and ribbons that tie in with the room's design theme. Wide mirrors reflect natural light and create an illusion of space in what is actually a long, narrow room.

Kitchen and Bath Association. Also check whether the estimate includes the cost of all fixtures and installation, plus the total renovation and decoration of the bathroom. In some cases, only installation work is done and the finishing touches are left up to you.

Costs can vary enormously, too, if you are quoted a price for plastic pipe as opposed to the traditional copper. In some cases the traditional materials may be necessary if they are to be connected to an old system or if period or reproduction items—where sizes can vary—are to be fitted.

Don't forget to plan the lighting at this stage. Arrange for any cable or wiring installation before the walls are tiled or decorated.

THE LOOK

The bathroom can be decorated in a number of ways. You can create a traditional bath-

room that includes a freestanding bathtub complete with ball-and-claw feet, a toilet with a pull-chain and wooden seat, and a large-size sink set into a washstand top. Reproductions of these old-fashioned bathroom units are available. Alternatively, you may want a Scandinavian bathroom, sauna-style with wood paneling throughout. Or possibly you would prefer a bathroom that doubles as a fitness center—an exercise bike, treadmill, and therapeutic massage bathtub can all be fitted into a large bathroom space.

Style   The style will depend on the size and shape of the room, the effect you want to create, and the fixtures you already have or are planning to install. If the bathroom is used by a family, there may have to be some degree of compromise where interests conflict. When the bathroom is in a suite with the master bedroom, it can echo the design and color scheme used in the bedroom.

Color   Color schemes for bathrooms can be more exciting and adventurous than in rooms where you spend more time. Bathrooms tend to be a little cold and clinical, and a warm ambience may be a great improvement. If you want a quiet or neutral scheme, all the right colors to enable you to achieve the correct atmosphere are available in bathroom fittings, tiles, and accessories. Cooperation between the manufacturers has ensured a good mix-and-match of accessories, such as blinds, shower curtains, and towels. Several of the bathroom manufacturers have collaborated to produce a coordinated range of fittings, with recommendations in their catalogs. Always check colors in the store or showroom, however, rather than relying on printed brochures.

Surfaces   As in the kitchen, surfaces need to be steam resistant, and if the room is prone to condensation problems, try to avoid too many shiny, cold surfaces. Washable wall coverings or matte or semi-matte paint can be combined with ceramic tiles. This makes a very flexible arrangement, since you can change wall coverings or paint more frequently than you will want to change or cover up the tiles. If you do decide on ceramic tiled walls, make sure you know what they will look like over the entire wall area. One of the most successful ways of designing the tiled area is to have part plain or textured tiles and part patterned, to form definite panels. Contrasting tiles can also be used in a border design to outline windows, baths, basins, or other important features. Alternatively, use plain tiles set on the diagonal and edge with the same plain tiles set straight. This looks very effective with brilliant white tiles in a well-lit bathroom.

The bathroom floor is a very important surface. Most people prefer a warm, soft floor covering but carpeting is not always practical in a bathroom that is used by a large family. Cushioned vinyl softened with washable cotton rugs is a practical compromise. Special wall-to-wall bathroom carpets that wear well are also available. They are comparatively inexpensive and can actually be taken up and washed. They have a waterproof rubber backing and dry quickly.

Lighting   The sink, shaving, and makeup area needs good direct light that shines on the face when seen in the mirror—the light fixture and mirror can be combined. Light the rest of the room with background lighting, with additional direct lighting for the bath in a large bathroom. Make sure lighting is adequate in the shower, with direct lighting if the shower is in a separate space. Illuminate the inside of any deep cupboards. Make sure that all fixtures are steam-, condensation-, and splash-proof, and that main lights are controlled by separate switches or controlled from outside the room.

Living and Dining Rooms

Lately, living and dining rooms in family homes have become more formal in style, and the kitchen has evolved as the heart of the house and the room from which the family room has evolved. The kitchen has become an informal cooking, eating, and sitting area that combines other functions as well. The living room may be used mainly by the adults, with the children using a more casual family room. If so, the furniture can be much more expensive, elegant, and fragile in the living room. Frequently, the dining room is still traditionally formal; however, it may now sometimes be used as a dual-purpose family room and eating area.

Furniture styles have changed too. Upholstered furniture, in particular, has acquired a completely new image, with much better, more interesting, and more comfortable designs often replacing the conventional three-piece set of one sofa and two armchairs. Many styles will fit into a variety of rooms and furnishing schemes, giving greater flexibility. Some special items of living room furniture, upholstered or cabinet style, are almost an art form in themselves and can be used as pieces of sculpture, highlighted with angled spotlights. They can provide a dramatic focal point and set the style of a room.

Living rooms often need to permit a variety of activities. This will mean very careful planning to create a comfortable and inviting room, at the same time accommodating the different functions.

Dining rooms are a different concept, because they have to contain certain items, such as a dining table, chairs, and some storage facilities. They may be formal in style, used only for entertaining and special occasions, or they may be used more frequently and include items that perform several functions. Sometimes living and dining rooms are combined in one main living area. Two styles can be juxtaposed here, so long as they are complementary, or one style can be adopted throughout.

PLANNING LIVING ROOMS

Your basic plan will depend on whether you are furnishing for the long term or whether you want a quick face-lift. It will also depend on whether there are any major or minor design faults that need improving. It pays to get the living room right at the start—if you have a comfortable, attractive room in which to relax and entertain, coping with other problem areas will be easier. Look at the room and its basic shape, and decide whether you are going to make any structural changes, such as opening up or removing a fireplace, altering or installing a window, or possibly restoring original features, including rebuilding walls.

Once you have considered improvements, you will need to plan the various areas and activities into which the room may have to be divided. The sitting area will be the most important. Plan this first for comfort and flexibility. The conventional sofa and armchairs may not suit your particular requirements or room shape. Unit seating, individual chairs, or two different-sized sofas are all possible alternatives. Unusual pieces of furniture can be unified by their upholstery or by the clever use of color and accessories.

The sitting area has to be functional, too, and must allow for watching television, listening to music, reading, or conversation. This may mean that some of the furniture needs to be easy to move around. Always try to zone the areas in a living room, particularly if it has to accommodate several activities, and keep the sitting areas away from the main traffic routes.

Make sure the items necessary for enjoying the room are stored in a practical and pleasing way. Books always look attractive on open shelves, but items such as records, cassettes, and videotapes are safer concealed behind doors.

If the dining area is part of the same room, but you do not want it to be too obvious, then look for compact furniture. For a room with a very limited space, a table that pulls out from a piece of storage equipment or one that folds back flat against the wall may be the perfect answer. Dining chairs can also be dual-purpose: They can be used as desk chairs, kept in the hall, be stackable, or even wall-hanging, in the tradition of the Shakers.

Storage items, such as glasses and cutlery, could be kept in the same cabinet used to store drinks. This, in fact, can make an ideal room divider, positioned to back the seating in the sitting area, facing the dining table. Zoning the areas visually in this way is very simple. There are also other, slightly more unusual ways: You can build a platform and raise the dining area slightly, sink the sitting area into a conversation area, or get semipermanent room dividers such as vertical louver blinds, screens, folding doors, or curtains. A change of floor covering—rugs, carpet, or tiles laid to outline features, or featuring a border effect—can also help create a feeling of separate entities without making the area seem cramped.

Lighting for living and dining areas needs to be flexible and functional, so part of the room can be darkened when not in use and so that various tasks can continue with the rest of the room bathed in a glow of background lighting. Also remember to install the necessary wiring and fixtures when doing any structural or preparation work, before you begin redecorating.

In the living room, in particular, since you are likely to want to sit and relax, you should try to remove or disguise any irritating features. If the room has a long blank wall, an unattractive window, or several different-shaped windows on one wall, or an ugly radiator, plan to disguise or possibly to remove or replace the feature before redecoration.

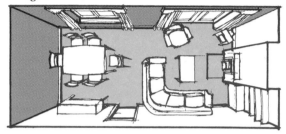

Living rooms need to be multipurpose, and fitting in all the furniture has to be cleverly planned within the constraints of the room's shape and size. Always try to zone the areas, so that the dining function is separated from sitting, listening, television, and study areas.

Long and narrow

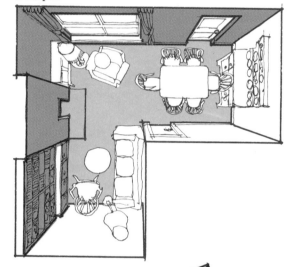

L-shaped

Square

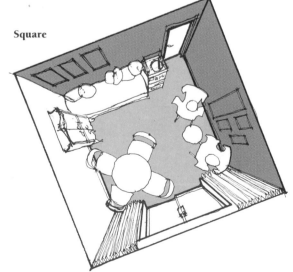

The curved shape of the seating units here adds interest to a long, narrow room, and forms a natural divider. Recesses to each side of the fireplace are fully utilized, and the dining area is flexibly furnished to provide extra space when needed.

This L-shaped room is furnished in traditional style so that the short, narrow part is used for dining, and the major section becomes the sitting and conversation area. There is no need to emphasize the natural division created by the shape.

Square rooms are harder to handle, since by their very nature they can appear boxlike and boring. Here a very small room has been adapted for sitting and dining. The table with four chairs grouped around it takes up one corner in front of the window. This furniture is light enough to be moved into another part of the house if the extra space is required for informal entertaining.

Insightful planning divides and defines this multipurpose room. The room has been zoned into distinct islands of activity that give it a sense of being a much larger space. One end is used for dining, another for sitting, and a third corner serves as a work space. Both the couch and the dining table and chairs are positioned in a way that makes the most of the New York City skyline. The black border of the rug creates a definite area and the reflective surfaces of the coffee table and the dining table foster the illusion of space, and at night must mirror the sparkling city skyline.

PLANNING DINING ROOMS

If the dining room is a separate room and you already have plenty of space in the home, then you will be able to plan for formal and informal dining. In many homes, however, the dining room does have to be dual-purpose, sometimes doubling as an office or workroom, which may make a very formal scheme impossible.

Planning a dining room is like planning a kitchen: It comes down to the eating patterns of the household. If you always eat together but generally gather around the kitchen table, you will occasionally want to have a more formal meal. If you have a family, the age and interests of the children will also influence planning—small children need very different dining facilities from teenagers. The type of entertaining you do, whether for friends or business colleagues, may influence the way the dining room is planned and styled.

If you are undecided about a plan for the dining area, think about your favorite restaurant and try to analyze its atmosphere. See if you can re-create some of that feeling in your

In another design scheme, the windows might have seemed severe, but in this situation, which favors the color black and the use of metal, the unadorned windows only reinforce those elements.

own home, especially the use of subtle lighting and creation of an intimate atmosphere.
Remember, however, that waiters are trained
to skirt around tables and chairs. In the home
you may well need much more space to circulate, to allow for chairs to be pulled away
from the wall or table, and for doors or drawers to be opened or closed.

Dining rooms and dining areas should be
planned in practical proximity to the kitchen,
possibly with a pass-through shelf when they
are next door to each other. If this is not feasible, then a serving trolley may be a good
buy.

THE LOOK

The style, color, and atmosphere of the living
and dining rooms will entirely depend on the
architectural style, the size and shape of the

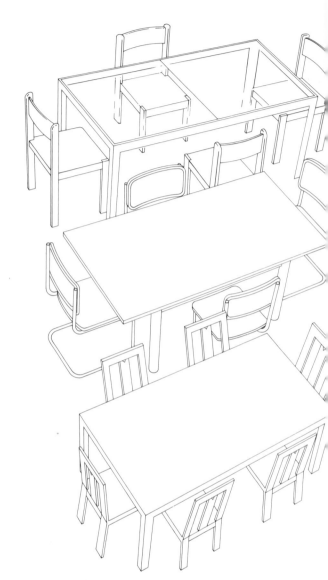

*Most formal entertaining takes place in the dining room,
whether it's business dinners, socializing with friends, or
family holiday dinners. If your home has enough space for
a formal dining room, invest it with a personality that will
make dining there a memorable event.*

*This traditional dining room would already have been
thought beautiful because of its pleasing proportions and
fine furnishings. The pale painted floor, with its drawn-on
birds and branches, adds a curious, whimsical perspective, and delicately ties together a theme of twigs and
leaves found in the curtain fabric and chandelier. The light
from that chandelier is reflected in and multiplied by a
large gilded mirror, over which a row of recessed ceiling
lights illuminates the room.*

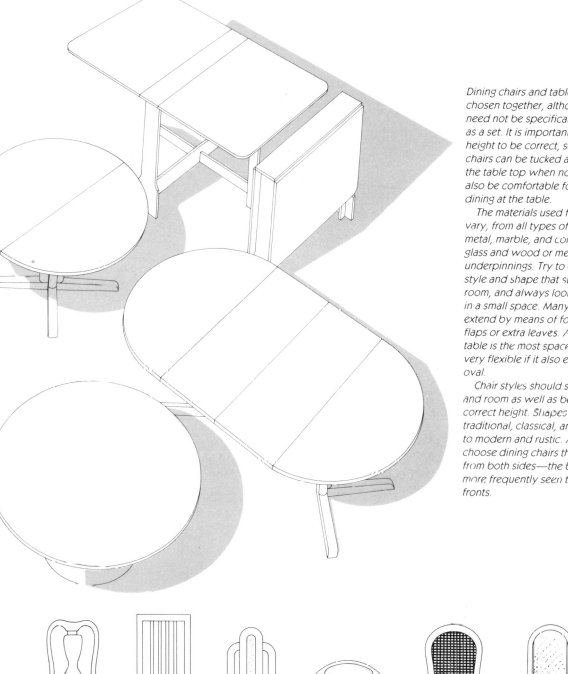

Dining chairs and tables should be chosen together, although they need not be specifically designed as a set. It is important for the height to be correct, so that the chairs can be tucked away under the table top when not in use, and also be comfortable for sitting and dining at the table.

The materials used for tables vary, from all types of wood to metal, marble, and combinations of glass and wood or metal underpinnings. Try to choose a style and shape that suits your room, and always look for flexibility in a small space. Many tables extend by means of fold-down flaps or extra leaves. A circular table is the most space-efficient and very flexible if it also extends to an oval.

Chair styles should suit the table and room as well as being the correct height. Shapes vary from traditional, classical, and Art Deco to modern and rustic. Always choose dining chairs that look good from both sides—the backs are more frequently seen than the fronts.

room, the type of furniture you want to use, and your life-style. All the different styles discussed in Section Four can be used successfully in the main living or dining area of the home.

Surfaces can also be much more flexible, depending on the type of room and the use it will get. A sitting room used by adults only can be designed to have pale carpets, fragile furnishings, and beautifully textured walls, but a living room for a family with pets needs more practical and long-lasting surfaces, par- ticularly the floor covering and upholstery. In this type of combined living-dining area, a washable floor covering such as linoleum or tile, laid throughout with a large rug to soften the sitting area, is a practical compromise.

Lighting   Lighting should be flexible in living-dining areas to allow for different activities. Control the background lighting with dimmer switches. You can do this in living areas by highlighting various decorative items or illuminating display shelves.

Family Rooms

A natural outgrowth of the kitchen is the family room, a combination cooking, eating, and sitting area that allows families with today's busy schedules to run in and out—to cook, eat, do homework—and still see one another. A family room may include other areas, such as a media center, home office, or laundry center, depending on the family and its needs. But the core of it is the same as it was in American Colonial homes, where it was called the "great" room—a kitchen, dining, and living room in one. Today, homes with family rooms most likely still have a living room and dining room for more formal occasions, but the family room is the most popular room in the house, because a range of activities can occur there simultaneously.

PLANNING THE FAMILY ROOM

In planning a family room, consider your options and needs. First your options: Do you have room to build an extension onto your house for a new room, or would it be easier to convert a few small rooms or possibly one larger one, such as the garage, into a family room? Figure out what is realistic for you.

Then consider your needs. What do you want the family room for? If you'd like to use it for informal entertaining, in addition to regular family use, you might want to include a counter to use for buffets, a good number of comfortable chairs, a wet bar, and possibly patio doors that lead to a deck or terrace. If you'd like a play area for small children, set aside a space where they can be safe and happy while you are in another part of the home attending to other things.

You can also arrange a space for studying, or a home office or library. Set up a wall of built-ins with desks, cabinets, and shelves for books and paper, and install task lighting. You may want to include a jack for a telephone and extra electrical outlets for a computer and other electronics. The family room is also a perfect place for a laundry center, where you can wash, fold, and iron while being in close proximity to the activity of the house. Or you can create a hobby center where a sewing machine, painting easel, or other materials for family hobbies can be used and stored. Of course, you won't want all these areas—just pick and choose what is best for you according to your life-style and desires.

Once you decide what you want and what your space will allow, put your plans on paper. Include all the details, such as electrical outlets, windows, closets, doors, and heat and ventilation ducts.

THE LOOK

A family room should be light and airy, with large windows, skylights, and patio or French doors, if possible, to let in sun. It should also be comfortable and inviting. A fireplace or intimate dining or reading spot helps to promote this look. Above all, the family room should be intimate, warm, relaxed, and fairly informal.

Style Family rooms are usually decorated in a "country casual" style. To enhance your choice of furniture to achieve this look, help the room along by adding moldings to doors and walls, running wallpaper borders at the ceiling or chair-rail level, keeping electronic equipment out of sight (perhaps in an old-fashioned armoire), and installing built-in cabinets that have the look of finely crafted furniture.

Family rooms, however, can take on any style. For example, a contemporary look can be created to complement the all-white kitchens that are popular today. A Colonial look that includes a stone fireplace would also be in keeping with the roots of the family room.

Color A family room can be any color desired, of course, but the standard colors of kitchens—light shades and neutrals—are often used because they are carried from the kitchen out to the other areas. Use color to connect the various spaces, whether it is bright primaries or the faded tones of denims. When one or two colors predominate, a space is unified.

Surfaces More than any other area in the house, surfaces in the family room need to be very practical. Because it is a place children and pets will probably frequent, you need easy-to-clean materials such as vinyl or polyurethaned wood floors, walls painted with scrubbable paint, casual furnishings in durable fabrics. And because it is a place where you may be entertaining, select furniture that is easy to care for.

Lighting A family room should be bright, for both practical and psychological reasons. Good lighting will make the space more comfortable, which is the aim of the room. Since there are so many activities going on in this one room, you'll need both task and overhead lighting. Put the overheads on a dimmer, and place switches in at least two locations in the room so you can control lighting from where you are at the moment.

Bedrooms

The bedroom is usually a highly personal room, and this should be reflected in its particular style and type of decor. Bedrooms come in all shapes and sizes—from master bedrooms possibly with a suite incorporating a dressing area or bathroom, to single rooms used mainly for sleeping, dual-purpose rooms that double as studies or offices, or children's rooms, which may double as play-rooms.

A bedroom needs to accommodate clothes, sports and hobby equipment, and personal items, as well as providing for sleep and relaxation. As in the kitchen, the bedroom storage space often has to be extensive; it is always wise to plan for much more storage area than you think you will need. If you are going to install any built-in furniture, you will need to do your own measuring and planning in advance, to ensure that you get exactly what you need.

The most important item of furniture in a bedroom, however, is not the storage unit but the bed. The choice is enormous: a dramatic four-poster, a romantic brass bed, a dual-purpose sofa bed, a water bed, a futon, a simple divan, or bunkbeds for children's rooms. The bed should be chosen to reflect the image of the room. If you want a traditional room, for example, look at headboards, and four-posters. Once you have made a decision, style the rest of the room around the bed.

The size of the bed will depend on the space available and your requirements. Always buy a bed or mattress from a reputable store or bedding specialist and try it out before you buy. This means actually lying full length on several different beds, with your head supported on a pillow, until you are quite sure you have chosen the most comfortable and suitable bed for you. If you are buying a bed for somebody else, take him or her along to try it out; in a shared situation, both partners should try the bed separately and together.

Beds, apart from being comfortable for the sleeper as far as firmness is concerned, must be wide enough and long enough. Beds come in certain standard sizes, but you can also get special widths, lengths, and different shapes to order.

It is important to check on the condition of a mattress after a few years' use. A mattress should be changed fairly regularly—after 20 years for superior mattresses and after 10 years for those of lesser quality. Make sure to test your spare beds occasionally, lest you subject guests to an uncomfortable night!

If you are planning a dual-purpose room, the sofa or studio bed should be adequate for both purposes. Simple sofas, made from foam slabs that open to make a bed, are comfortable for occasional overnight use but are not suitable for sleeping every night. If you need a convertible sofa that is to be used daily for sitting and nightly for sleeping, look for one with a separate mattress and a wire or sprung base hidden inside. A divan bed with a tailored cover or throw covering can be appropriate for day and night use, but it does need a firm sprung base for long-term comfort.

There are other beds suitable for dual-purpose use, including ones that fold up into a cupboard or even convert into a coffee table or other piece of furniture. Except for the fold-up (Murphy) bed, which can be used nightly, these are best for occasional use.

PLANNING BEDROOMS

Most bedrooms today are used for a number of activities besides sleeping, including the storage of clothes and other items, so your scheme for this room should be worked out carefully on graph paper. With a child's room, you have to allow for growing and changing needs (see pages 71–74). In planning rooms for other people, try to think ahead as well, and plan for future needs.

Many bedrooms contain suitable places for

This traditional bedroom is planned around a four-poster bed and fairly traditional accessories. The room is softened with floor-length curtains and enough bed drapery, styled to look like mosquito netting, to have it comfortably fit into the home of an Englishman who has spent some years in India. Further Anglo-Raj details include intricately carved furniture, a wicker table and chair, and the framed picture of a turbaned man. The room's comfortable overstuffed look and its interesting furnishings and accessories compensate for its lack of architectural details. Overhead light filtered through sheer bed drapery gives the room a soft, diffused glow.

storage. There might be recesses on either side of a fireplace (or other projection) that could contain fitted cabinets, or a cabinet could be built on one side and built-in shelves on the other. If the recesses are not very deep, the cabinets could be built to project slightly and be joined to shelves or a dressing table. If you do not want anything too permanent, put adjustable shelves and hanging clothes rods in the recesses, and use pull-down shades, Roman blinds, or curtains with a valance to cover it.

A long wall may be a natural place to install a whole row of cabinets, leaving an alcove in the center for the headboard of the bed. The closets can be linked with high cabinets or shelves that go across the gap, allowing space for concealed lighting below. Alternatively, use the space for a picture or a mirror.

If the room is large, it may be possible to build cabinets, shelving and other storage out from the wall, at right angles to it, dividing the room into sleeping and dressing areas. The headboard can be placed at the back of the row of cabinets, and the cabinets can be decorated to match the room, or covered with wood or fabric. If you do not want to form such a permanent division, but you like

Since it serves an architectural function, this bed's headboard was covered with wood by the designer and decorated with molding, so that it looks like the wainscotting portion of a wall. The headboard, like a wall, also divides the room into sleeping and sitting areas. Positioned facing the window, the bed takes close-up advantage of the view. Striped wallpaper, which matches the green-and-white striped ticking of the bed skirt, gives the bedroom the illusion of height. Curtains would only make the small windows look smaller and shorter, so the windows are fitted with vertically striped shades.

the idea of zoning the areas, use a curtain, lace or fabric panel, or vertical blinds to separate sleeping and dressing areas. Where two children are sharing the room, it is often better to give them separate halves and make each of them responsible for their own part. Dividing with wardrobes, chests, and other storage furniture can work well here, and blinds can be used to close any gaps.

MASTER BEDROOM

If the room is for two adults, a flexible approach to storage and planning is even more important and may not necessarily mean dividing everything up. The master bedroom,

for example, is usually the largest bedroom in a home.

Some master bedrooms, especially in large suburban houses, are complete suites that are designed to meet all the needs of sleeping, dressing, and bathing comfortably in one large, convenient space. They are designed to be lived in, with sitting areas, TV corners, and small offices common. These suites can also be created by combining two smaller bedrooms into one, or by converting part of an adjoining room or landing.

Coordinating designs of fabric, wallpaper, bed linens, and bath accessories make it simple to create an attractive bedroom–sitting room suite that doesn't necessarily have to be expensive. For example, sheets today are so sophisticated in design that they can be used to cover chairs, divans, and small sofas in the master suite and complement or match the overall design. And beds are better dressed than ever, with endless accessories such as dust ruffles, pillow covers, and layers of sheets and spreads to make the striking focal point of the room and set the tone for luxury and relaxation.

Do try to plan for somewhere to sit and relax in a large bedroom. A comfortable corner, with chairs, a small table and light for reading or sewing, and shelves of books against the wall can be the perfect spot to "get away." If space does not allow for a sitting area, it is sometimes possible to position a small settee or chaise longue parallel with the bottom of a double bed.

A mini-office can also be useful in a large master bedroom—a desk can add an attractive piece of furniture to the overall design. A television set can be positioned inside a wall-mounted cupboard, on top of a bureau, or concealed behind a door.

Although the master bedroom is usually the main bedroom in a home, the largest bedroom may be given over to the children as a combined bedroom/playroom. It may also make an excellent "granny apartment" for an elderly relative, perhaps with a separate entrance to the house. Then too, if you work from home, this room may have to become the office or studio and double as a guest or even main bedroom. Always think about a room's function and plan carefully to make maximum use of its size and shape.

Lofts and Storage

If your bedrooms have high ceilings, you can also plan heightwise. It may be practical,

for example, to incorporate a loft or sleeping platform on top of built-in furniture. You could also install a closet, small office, or other facilities under a loft bed. You will need to make detailed room plans (see pages 10–11) to work out the exact proportions.

Do not discount the space over the bed in rooms with normal height ceilings—it is sometimes possible to mount storage units on the ceiling above the bed. They will need to be firmly screwed into the ceiling and can be used for "dead" storage. You could also conceal lighting and suspend curtains or drapes from the units to simulate a four-poster bed. You could run a shelf right around the bedroom above the level of the curtain rail, excluding the wardrobe wall. You could also run a hanging rail under the shelf to provide additional space for clothes and bags. Match the color of the shelf and rail with other items of furniture.

To plan practically, work out exactly what you need on graph paper in the usual way, remembering to allow for opening doors and drawers, moving around the furniture, and pulling out the bed for making. Remember that bunk beds can be very heavy to move. If you are going to call in a firm of experts to design and make the furniture, they will probably make scale drawings themselves, but it pays to have done your own homework so that you can brief them properly.

The Look

Bedrooms can be decorated in many different styles to create the required atmosphere. Again, the main emphasis should be provided by color and pattern, but the furniture you select will also dictate the chosen look to some extent. Any built-in or storage furniture should be in keeping with the overall decorating theme, or should be treated so that it blends in with the existing decor. If the storage units are attractive in themselves, they can even become the focal point of the room.

Color   Color will help to foster the right atmosphere and can be chosen to relax or stimulate, make a room more intimate or cozy, or create a room that is spacious and elegant. In most bedrooms, accessories are again important and can help a great deal toward achieving the finished look. Bed linens in particular can coordinate or contrast with the scheme and should be chosen carefully as an integral part of the room's furnishings. A bed cover can transform a room during the day, for example. If the bedding is designed to be seen, choose several different designs and colors for variety. Cool pastel colors can look refreshing and light in summer, and strong, warmer ones will seem cozy in winter.

Surfaces   Fabrics and carpeting used in the bedroom usually tend to be softer, more luxurious than elsewhere, but it depends on whose room it is. An adult bedroom may be decorated in pale colors and have high-pile carpeting because it will be treated carefully, whereas a child's or teenager's room will need tough, washable surfaces and practical colors.

Lighting   Light the dressing table, makeup area, vanity unit, or dressing area with direct lighting, independently switched. Light the bed area with well-shaded direct bedside or wall-mounted lamps, one for each side of the bed in a shared bedroom. You can check the height for the light fixtures by sitting in a comfortable reading position and angling the light to shine on the open page of a book. The room can be lit generally with subdued back-

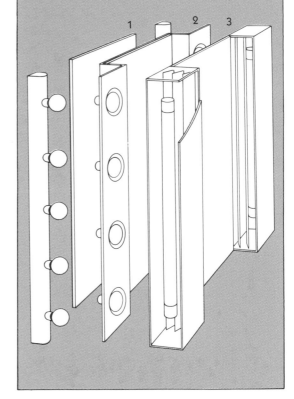

LIGHTING FOR DRESSING TABLES

Lighting units for dressing tables and bathroom vanities need to be strong and clear for shaving and putting on makeup. The light should shine onto the face, but not into the eyes. Theatrical-style bulbs surrounding a mirror or running down either side provide a good light (1, 2). Fluorescent strips down each side or across the top and bottom of the mirror will also light the face clearly (3). For a softer glow, use several narrow strip lights, filtered through a louvered panel.

ground lighting on a dimmer switch, controlled from both the door and the bed. Light the insides of any deep storage units or wardrobes, with the switch fitted to the doorjamb. In a dual-purpose bedroom, include direct lighting for a study or hobby area.

ROOMS TO GROW UP IN

Today more than ever before, children's rooms are recognized as an important part of the home—the one place in the house that is a child's own, a place for self-expression. Varied, colorful, and fun products for children's rooms—from washable wall paint to furnishings to smart safety features—are widely available and make it a pleasure to decorate a room for a child or to help the child do it.

Planning, designing, and furnishing rooms for children *can* be a challenge, however. The different stages of a child's early years usually mean different furnishings and decor, and it is important to plan a room from the start that allows for expansion and change.

Do not immediately rush out to fill the room with furniture. Think carefully about the overall plan before you start. Consider having certain pieces of furniture made to order; the versatility, high quality, and convenience of custom-designed units are often well worth the extra cost. A built-in cupboard, for example, can be designed to last from birth to high school—adjustable shelves and hanging space should make this possible.

Free-standing furniture can be selected from a line that can be added to later on. Check to make sure that there will be a continuity of supply for at least a few years. You may find the most practical way of planning is to start out with the final stage and work backward.

Infancy The needs of a baby are relatively simple, so the nursery should be a pleasant and practical room for the parents as well. In addition to a crib, the room should include a unit to store essentials plus a changing table and bathing area. A rocking chair will give the parents somewhere to sit when feeding the infant, and it is worth considering installing an intercom system, linked to the downstairs rooms or master bedroom, so that you can hear when the baby cries.

SAFETY HINTS FOR CHILDREN'S ROOMS

Children's rooms should be practical and pretty, but above all safe. At each stage of development there are new hazards.

- Check all windows for safety. Sash windows are usually safe, but most other types, particularly casement and pivoting windows, can be a hazard. If necessary, fit bars (a legal requirement in a number of cities in the United States).
- Equip electrical outlets with outlet covers or plugs so the child cannot poke anything into the sockets. Position light switches where the child can reach them easily.
- Remove any inside bolts or keys from a child's door (do this also in the bathroom while a child is very young).
- Make sure furniture is safe and there is no possibility of pulling over tall dressers, shelves, or stacked items. Use brackets or wall mounting to prevent this from happening. If the furniture is painted, make sure the paint is nontoxic and safe; special nursery paints are available for walls and furniture.
- Make sure cribs and playpens conform to government requirements—this means safe sides and ends with bars spaced so that the child cannot push his/her head through.
- The floor should be a safe play area. Use smooth, washable flooring, and avoid slippery rugs or ones that turn up at the corners.

Apart from the specific items of nursery equipment, the room can be designed to be adapted later to an older child. Decorate everything very simply at this stage and avoid too many cuddly toy motifs. Keep the furniture plain; add patterns in wall coverings, curtains, or attractive nursery borders that can easily be changed when needed. An easy-care flooring such as vinyl softened by washable rugs is the best treatment underfoot.

The toddler   At this stage, the child becomes mobile and wants play space. A low bed, toy box, high chair and playpen may all become necessary. Remove the rocking chair for the parents and any baby equipment. The decorations may well be altered at this time, and a pull-down window shade that blocks out the light can be added to help the toddler sleep on light summer evenings. This and the next stage of childhood involve a good deal of cleanup, so store the rugs.

The kindergarten child   At this age, the child usually needs a dual-purpose room, a bedroom-playroom. It should include a play area, a space to feel free to make a mess with paints or hobbies. Bunk beds are a sensible choice if the room is to be shared with another child. The decorations may change slightly to involve the favorite cartoon or TV character of the moment. A change of curtains or fresh wallpaper will probably be sufficient to create the desired effect.

The school child   School-age children usually have quite strong ideas about how their rooms should look. By this time, real hobbies and interests have developed, which may mean storage for bulky sports equipment. A desk and bookshelves and improved clothing storage are required, and the decorative scheme may have to be changed again. At this stage the flooring could be changed, depending on the room and the child's activities. Practical possibilities include carpeting or area rugs.

The preteen child   The older child usually wants a room where friends can come to chat, work, read, and play. Technology is likely to influence this age group (computers may be the most important "toy"), so a large desk and lots of power outlets are needed. At this age too, definite ideas on decoration, furniture, and design may begin to emerge. These should be encouraged and the child should help make the decisions, perhaps even to try a hand at some supervised decorating. Lots of storage space will also be essential.

The infant
The room is really a nursery at this stage, requiring comfortable changing facilities and washable floor surfaces, softened by rugs.

The toddler
A safe room where the child can make a mess. The crib is exchanged for a small bed, the rocking chair goes and is replaced by a playpen, the bassinet gives way to a high chair.

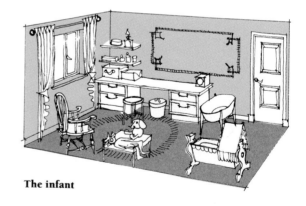

The infant

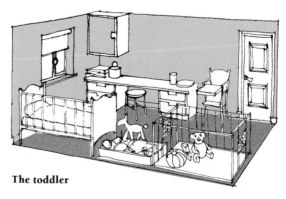

The toddler

The teenager The teen years will probably call for a total change of scene. Teens may need a sofa bed that can also be used for friends who sleep over. Remember though, that the mattress must be firm and suitable for both sitting and sleeping. A futon might be the answer; or you may be able to compromise with tailored covers and cushions on a low divan bed. Floor cushions also are a good idea for extra seating. Don't be alarmed if the decorations change drastically—your child may prefer a black, star-studded ceiling; garish posters may appear on the walls; disco lighting may replace more conventional fixtures.

The Looks

The colors and accessories of a child's room are a changing theme throughout the child's developmental years. Small children like bright colors, so starting with a pastel nursery and then adding color in accents is one approach. Brighter colors and treatments could be added as the room becomes a playroom-bedroom, and then as the room becomes a complete living area for the

The kindergarten child
Plenty of play space is now needed. The bed is replaced and the changing area becomes a play-desk-painting surface. A blackboard is situated on one wall.

The school child
The desk area is adapted again and a cabinet is added to provide more storage. A large toy box doubles as sitting and play space.

The preteen child
A drop-down table top is located next to the desk, which has TV and computer facilities. A small table is added and the bed gets a tailored cover.

The teenager
Storage for clothes and hobbies now becomes a priority. The storage system is streamlined and the room takes on the air of a sophisticated bedroom.

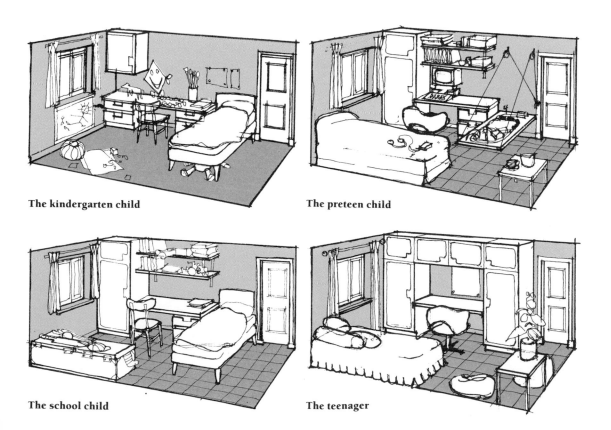

The kindergarten child

The preteen child

The school child

The teenager

Besides housing the basic equipment babies need, the nursery should be a practical, pleasing room for parents. Decorate everything simply at this stage and add patterns in wall coverings, curtains, or wallpaper borders that can easily be changed later. This nursery makes the most of a small space by employing a very pale color scheme; pale, light-filtering curtains and soft furnishings; and a bleached wooden floor.

Adaptability is a key element to consider when designing a child's room. Simple furnishings and a simple color scheme serve as a suitable backdrop for the inevitable changes to come. In this room, it's easy to imagine the children's books and toys being replaced with a stereo system and a collection of posters. Take away the toy airplane and top wallpaper border, substitute something contemporary and geometric, and the room will have a more grown-up look.

A bunk bed arrangement maximizes play space in this older child's bedroom. It also makes the room suitable for the addition of a sibling or the possibility of a sleepover.

fashionable teenager, coordinated wall coverings and accessories can develop a new look.

Style   The style of the room will depend on the child's age and interests. With children's rooms the question of specific styling does not arise in quite the same way as it does for other rooms in the house. The particular tastes of the room's owner will dictate the style.

Surfaces   Children's rooms above all need to be practical, particularly during infancy and early childhood. Washable flooring,

sponge-clean surfaces on furniture, washable woodwork, and walls papered with vinyl-coated wallpaper are the wisest choices for the first four stages.

Because of the need for constant change and updating to keep up with a child's needs, it is often more economical to keep the main surfaces of the room as plain as possible, and to introduce different designs in wallpaper borders on the plain-painted walls. Alternatively, a wall covering with a striking design can be introduced on perhaps one wall only, or in the curtains, pull-down shades, bed linens, and other accessories that can be easily changed when they are outgrown.

Dual-Purpose Rooms

In many houses and apartments, the shortage of space means a spare bedroom is an unlikely luxury. Any extra room has to be multifunctional, not just dual-purpose, and some large rooms become complete living areas. If a room is to double as an office and bedroom, and it is only to be used occasionally for overnight guests, it should be planned primarily for the main function. Multipurpose furniture here is ideal, but it is essential to remember when choosing sofa beds that if they will be slept on only rarely, they should be comfortable to sit on. If they are to be slept on every night, then they must be firm and comfortable as both bed and sofa. A futon is often a practical solution here. Wooden bases for futons come in a variety of styles and colors, and can easily be blended in with the overall color scheme.

In some cases the main living area may be the only place to put up a guest overnight. Again, convertible furniture should be selected primarily for seating comfort. A separate dining room can also be used as a sewing and TV room. In the bedroom-playroom, you can make bunk beds, platform beds, or colored scaffolding serve as part of the play area. Some fantasy furniture is available for children's rooms—beds and bunks shaped like space ships, buses, and Cinderella's coach—which can be converted later into chests of drawers and dressing tables. Before selecting such units, though, consider their practical aspects and probable lifespan in your child's room.

In larger homes, there may be a room that is used for many different purposes, such as a games and billiards room, an office or studio, a music room, a gym or workout room, or a sewing and crafts area.

PLANNING MULTIPURPOSE ROOMS

Designing a multipurpose room is more complex than planning almost any other room in the home. You will need to combine practical storage areas with comfortable, functional, and attractive furnishings and facilities. Carefully scaled plans, to see how everything fits in, are a must.

Consider the basic shape and size of the room and decide exactly what you want to accommodate in the way of furniture and storage, as well as the various activities for which the room will be used. What is the main function of the room? Give this your top priority, fitting other requirements around it.

If the room is to be an office but must also double as a spare bedroom, try to provide a storage unit that includes space for hanging guests' clothes. Select a desk that can also serve as a dressing table, and combine storage for files with drawers suitable for clothes. Choose a coffee table that can become a bedside table and will allow enough space for a sofa or divan to open out for sleeping. Folding tables can also be useful in an office or study. The table can serve as surface, desk, or drawing board, but can be folded away neatly when not needed.

Hobbies When a multifunctional room is also used for serious hobbies, then the furniture and surface treatments will center around that particular activity. Some hobbies can be messy, such as painting, pottery, woodwork, and metalwork, and require adequate equipment, such as an easel, kiln, workbench, or lathe. If this is the case, the equipment will take up some room and may be heavy. You will also need to bring in some hefty materials occasionally, so try to select a room on the ground floor for this purpose.

Other hobbies may require fireproof room furnishings or coverings, and some could involve installing adequate soundproofing to protect neighbors and other family members from noise. Consider this very carefully at the beginning of your decorating project and, if necessary, seek professional advice.

If a room is to be used as a music room, and perhaps doubles as a spare bedroom or study, it may have to accommodate a piano. Upright pianos are not too difficult to conceal behind screens, blinds, or curtains if you do not want them to be an integral part of the furnishing scheme. A grand or baby grand piano is more difficult to disguise. Try making it a focal point instead. A large exotic shawl or a patchwork quilt in flamboyant 1920s style thrown over it will both cover and protect it. Upright pianos can be decorated in any of the painted techniques to give them a newer look. If a music room needs a large collection of sound equipment and sophisticated electronics, make sure these are housed in a place that is safe, both from dust and from curious people. Soundproofing will be essential in such a room.

If a room is to accommodate a major game such as table tennis, the table will take up a lot of space, so think about the types that can be folded up and put away. In a smaller room that doubles as a guest room, stacking beds under the table when they are not in use might be practical. A hammock can easily be used, especially if a room is decorated to match in nautical or tropical style. In a taller room, a bed built onto a loft or platform will

Realizing how much time is spent in the kitchen, more families are choosing to plan kitchen-family rooms. In some houses this requires adding on or annexing a room, but in others it may just be a matter of rearranging furniture. In this kitchen the traditional kitchen table and chairs were forsaken for a counter, which also has a built-in oven and generous work surfaces. The space saved was given to a comfortable couch and two armchairs.

leave space underneath to accommodate a piano, game table, small office, or other essential furniture.

Note that any of these dual or multipurpose rooms will need specialized lighting and possibly extra electrical outlets. Billiards tables, for example, usually have overhead screened lighting. Desks and drawing boards need direct lighting, perhaps using angled lamps. Think about all these relationships as you devise your overall furnishing and storage plan.

ONE-ROOM LIVING

This type of room is definitely multipurpose and has to be planned as such. In a studio or loft consisting of one big room, the bed may be up in a loft or on a platform. When planning rooms for living, eating, sleeping, entertaining, and perhaps cooking and working in as well, consider the requirements of the person who will use the room most; you'll need to work out the most streamlined design to

As the center of activity, a kitchen is also a good place from which to manage the house, so it makes sense to include an office. With a kitchen office like this, a person could balance the checkbook, check the agenda for next week's appointments, and plan tomorrow's dinner party, all while watching something simmer on the stove. The office is neatly tucked into a corner of this eat-in kitchen and painted white so that it does not take up any visual space.

accommodate all the necessary features.

Splitting a "tall" room by raising the bed on a platform and installing a storage unit or a desk underneath is a good way of getting in all the necessary items. In a room with a ceiling of normal height you could build a platform to accommodate the mattress or bed, then use the space underneath for storage. In a study or work environment, low filing cabinets and storage drawers can be used to form the base of the platform. Look at the range of office and industrial furniture now available: It is often more practical, stronger, and less expensive than domestic furniture. If you select this type of furniture, you can decorate in

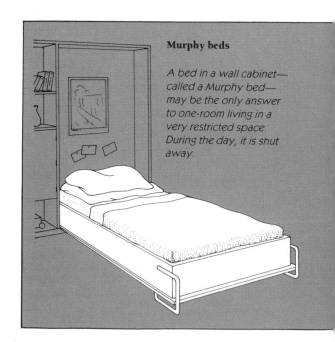

Murphy beds

A bed in a wall cabinet—called a Murphy bed—may be the only answer to one-room living in a very restricted space. During the day, it is shut away.

Sofa beds

Sofa or studio beds come in many shapes, sizes, and styles. Some simply unfold to form a base and mattress (single or double), while others have a folding base spring and mattress hidden inside the seat of the sofa, which is easily pulled out to form a double bed.

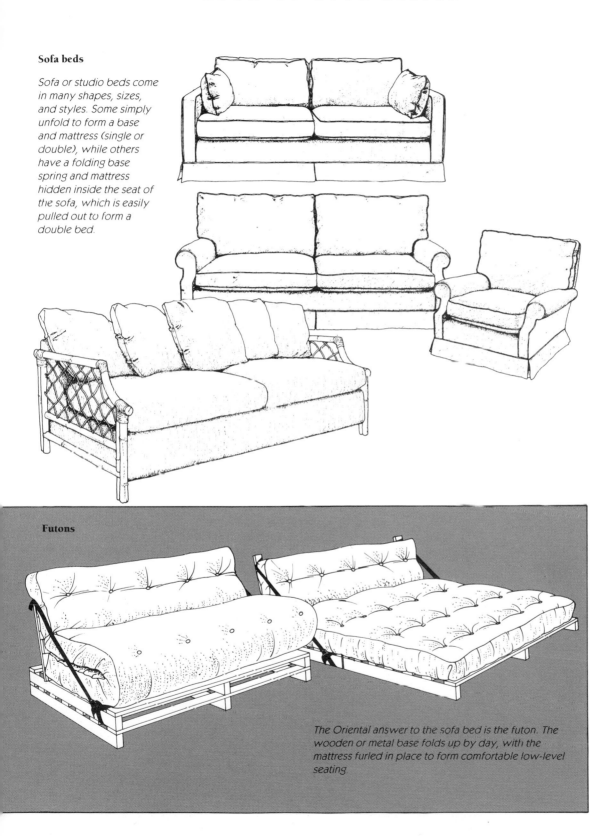

Futons

The Oriental answer to the sofa bed is the futon. The wooden or metal base folds up by day, with the mattress furled in place to form comfortable low-level seating.

Many city dwellers live in one-room studio apartments. Fitting every aspect of your life into one room requires creative and often unconventional thinking. This studio apartment, besides offering a sleeping, living, and dining area, also has room for a guest. A fold-up bed is inconspicuously tucked into a cabinet when not in use.

a bright, high-tech style. Murphy beds, which fold out from the wall, and sofabeds are also good options.

Often a divan bed can double as a sofa in dual-purpose and one-room living areas, placed parallel to the wall and with a tailored cover, a collection of cushions along the back, and bolster cushions on each side to form "arms." Or a bed can be covered with a colorful rug, Oriental-style, and piled high with exotic-looking cushions. Always make sure that a bed used in this way is of good quality, and firm-edged enough for sitting and sleeping.

When planning such a room on paper—always an essential exercise—remember to allow space for people to walk around the furniture and to use it, to open drawers and doors, or to pull back chairs from tables or desks.

THE LOOK

Since the main problem with multipurpose and one-room living areas is lack of space both in reality and visually, it is good to keep the shapes in larger areas simple and streamlined. Unnecessary clutter will minimize the available space. Mirrors can help to magnify the apparent size of a very small room, so use them cleverly, perhaps on the front of a row of cabinets along one wall, or as a panel in the darkest area to reflect light as well. Paneling the backs of doors with mirrors is another alternative. Even if the room is not very large, try at least to zone the areas visually, but avoid heavy dividers. You can zone the room by a change of floor covering or by a change of levels or by the way you arrange the furniture.

Style   Always follow basic styling principles with this type of room. With so much furniture to include, it can easily become a design disaster.

Color   In a room with limited space, a simple, neutral scheme works well, with color accents provided by accessories. Monochromatic schemes based on different values of one color also come into their own in this situation. Do not change the color scheme or decorations too abruptly from area to area, but use coordinated ranges to give one large living and sleeping area two distinct personalities. But color and pattern will need to be chosen to suit the purpose of the room too: brighter and more stimulating ones for children or young people's rooms or game rooms, and more restrained ones for rooms that are used for sleeping and relaxing. Color accents, added in the form of accessories, can also be increased. One set can be used for the main purpose of the room—when it is an office, for example—and changed for another set when it takes on its second function, such as entertaining.

Surfaces   Surfaces here will probably get harder wear than in other rooms, so they need to be tough and practical. The flooring in a game room, or where a hobby is really messy, should be similar to what you would put into the kitchen—quarry tiles, linoleum, or vinyl flooring—but it can be softened with rugs. Upholstery will take rougher treatment too, and two sets of tailored or loose covers may be more practical than fixed fabric. Furniture surfaces and walls should be washable.

Lighting   In a dual-purpose room, the lighting is determined by the different functions of the room. Make sure any desk area is adequately lit. You probably need a direct light that should come from behind and above for a computer or other keyboard. Install subdued background lighting and suitable direct lighting for reading and other tasks. Storage areas, files, and bookshelves should also be functionally lit, using separate controls.

Tricks of the Light

All too often, the way a room is lit is considered only at the final stages of decoration, when the accessories are added. Light fixtures and lamps are often thought of as accessories, and lamps in particular can be finishing touches, but the light source, its position and all wiring, should be decided upon at the planning stage.

Lighting can be used in many ways: to emphasize and enhance a feature, to dramatize or minimize the mode of decoration, or even to alter the shape of a room. Like color and pattern, lighting is an interior design tool that can be used to create atmosphere and style with maximum effect.

BASIC TYPES OF LIGHTING

There are three basic types of lighting; most rooms will have two, if not all three, types.

Background lighting A soft level of light throughout an area is particularly important in living areas and bedrooms, often in halls, stairs, and landing areas, and adds an extra dimension in kitchens and bathrooms. The level of background lighting can be further controlled with dimmer switches.

Direct or task lighting Focused illumination for the various jobs around the home is provided by direct lighting. It is essential in the kitchen for lighting up food preparation surfaces, the stove, the sink, and the laundry area; in the bathroom for shaving and applying makeup; in the bedroom for dressing tables and reading in bed; in offices for working at a desk; in the living area for reading; in the nursery for changing the baby; in the hall, stair, or landing area for illuminating stair treads and risers and telephone or closet areas.

Decorative or accent lighting Use it to "shape" the room or draw attention to a particular area or feature in a room. It may emphasize a collection of beautiful objects, illuminate a painting or a group of paintings, or spotlight a selection of houseplants or a piece of sculpture.

All three types of lighting should be as flexible as possible. Living rooms will need attractive as well as functional lighting. You may find you need more lighting than you originally thought, so allow for enough electrical receptacles when making a lighting plan.

LIGHTING IN PRACTICE

There are various ways of supplying the different types of lighting. Background illumination can be provided by lighting concealed behind window valances, subdued lighting incorporated in display shelves, ceiling light fixtures, crown molding, recessed ceiling lights, or illuminated panels in the ceiling. Lighting can be concealed behind moldings.

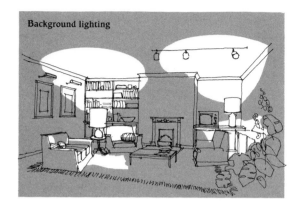

Background lighting

Direct or task lighting

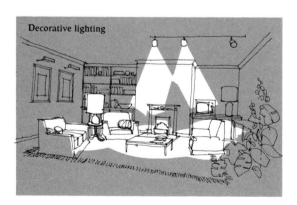

Decorative lighting

This living room is lit flexibly, with separate controls, to provide good illumination for all functions. Background lighting is provided by pools of light thrown up and down from table lamps. Direct or task lighting comes from spots, strategically placed on ceiling-mounted track. Decorative lighting floods pictures from special picture lights, individually mounted.

It also can be bounced off the ceiling by up-lights or lamps; wall lights; recessed fixtures set into the floow, wall, or ceiling; or uplights positioned to illuminate and shine through glass-topped tables or plant stands.

Direct lighting can be supplied by table, floor, or desk lamps; spotlights trained on a particular area; fluorescent, incandescent tubes, or circular fittings; strip lights or bulbs positioned above or around a mirror. It can also be provided by downlights strategically positioned over baths, sinks, or wall-mounted light fixtures over a bed.

Decorative or accent lighting is usually provided by spotlights. These can be individual, or grouped together and mounted on a ceiling or wall-mounted track, and include wallwashers (a type of floodlight), pinhole or framing projectors, and uplights and downlights. Even candles provide accent lighting.

Some fixtures can perform several func-

Direct or task lighting is essential in the kitchen for illuminating work surfaces. A hanging lamp is the most common form of ceiling lamp and the height at which it's hung and the type of shade will affect the intensity of the light it gives. Light is supplied in this kitchen by recessed ceiling lights and low-hanging task lighting. The shades are clear glass, permitting maximum light that is reflected on the glossy wooden counter surfaces.

In this living room two kinds of lighting are used: A lamp provides background lighting, and decorative lighting is used over a plant. In the mirrored panels of a screen you can see that decorative lighting is also used over a painting and a dried-flower arrangement on the opposite wall. With the blinds closed, the panels reflect the room's various forms of lighting, making up for some of the lost daylight.

tions and give a more flexible arrangement in a room where the lighting may have to be limited to a few different sources. In the initial stages, try to take as practical an approach to lighting as possible, seeing it as both functional and decorative.

Industrial lighting is worth considering. Curved and shaped tubes can be used to outline a picture or piece of sculpture, and a colored neon tube can appear playful or daring in the right setting.

TYPES OF FIXTURES

Recent developments in the lighting industry have led to some confusion over the names and purposes of a wide variety of electrical equipment. The amount of light supplied by conventional sources and the wattage of light bulbs necessary for the different types of fixtures vary, so check carefully the information attached to any fixtures you buy.

Lighting Specific Items

You will not necessarily have something specific to display and illuminate in every room although a softly glowing light on display shelves or a light shined on a curtain fabric to highlight the design can provide attractive background lighting. The accent lighting should be looked at in relation to the

TYPES OF LIGHTING

Once you have decided on the type of lighting you require and roughly where it will be located, light fittings have to be selected. Function as well as style has to be considered. Lighting stores and departments display a bewildering selection but are a good place to choose basic items. If you need advice, either call in a lighting design expert or go to a lighting supplier.

Spotlights and tracks

Freestanding lamps

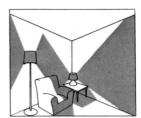

Hanging lights

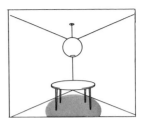

Desk lamps

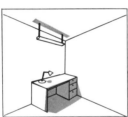

Desk lamps can be freestanding or clip-on. They provide concentrated areas of light and should be adjustable so that the fall of light can be altered.

Spotlights can be either mounted directly onto ceilings or walls or into track systems. They can be used as accent lighting to highlight objects or pictures, or as angled light in a work area—for example, directed at the stove, sink, and food preparation areas in the kitchen. A spot may be designed to hold an ordinary bulb or a special spot bulb with an internal silvered reflector for intensity; or the spot itself may house a low-voltage transformer that will cast a narrow beam of light onto a specific item.

Tracks offer a flexible approach to lighting. They can be fixed across the ceiling or down the wall. Light beams can be crossed at steep angles so that people in the room do not look directly into the beam of light.

A number of freestanding lamps around the room can be equipped with dimmer switches and provide very flexible background light. Lamp shades can be selected to cast the required amount of light and to control its intensity, as well as being decorative accessories in their own right. Directional light for reading can be provided by adjustable table lamps.

A hanging light situated in the center of the ceiling is the most common form of ceiling light. The height at which the shade is hung and the type of shade will affect the intensity of the light. A larger shade will tend to cast a softer and more subtle light.

Hanging lights provide good general light, but they tend to flatten shadows and divide a room, throwing light halfway down the walls.

They are very useful over a dining table, particularly if a rise-and-fall fixture is used.

Uplights

Uplights can be used to create very interesting shadow effects in a room. They can be positioned behind plants, beneath glass shelves, or in corners. They can also be directed to highlight objects or pictures dramatically.

Downlights

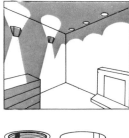

Downlights are metal canisters that can be recessed or semirecessed into ceilings to cast pools of light. Using either a spot bulb or a floodlight can provide either a concentrated circle of light or a wider pool of light.

Downlights can make color more brilliant and molding more effective, but they need to be carefully positioned. Use sparingly in the sitting room, where table lamps provide a cozier feel. Downlights are particularly suitable for large hall or stairwell areas to highlight objects of interest and provide a bright source of light.

room as a whole, and each fixture should be individually controlled to avoid a glaringly bright effect when all the lighting is switched on at once.

Some objects, such as pieces of sculpture, require specialized lighting so that the shadows and interplay of light emphasize the form rather than detract from it. It may be necessary to experiment until you get exactly the right light. The same may be true of a single object on a shelf, or a large single picture. It is possible to use lights with clips on a long cord to work out the best positions for any light fixtures. If you have an extensive or very special or valuable collection of some type, it could be worthwhile calling in an expert lighting designer. In fact, if you want any specialized lighting for a gallery or complicated exterior floodlighting for garden, patio, or swimming pool, it may be wise to call in an expert, ideally at the planning stage.

To light a single picture or wall hanging, conventional picture lights are easy to install but tend to light only the top area of a large painting. Spotlights, either single and angled or mounted on tracks, work well but can cause glare on the glass. Downlights recessed in the ceiling above or uplights placed below can also give good illumination. For an excellent direct light, consider a framing projector. With a wall hanging, where texture is all important, direct light can flatten and distort the effect. Try lighting it from the side or from below or above instead.

To light a group of pictures, the system may need to be different because there may be a larger wall area and possibly an unusual shape to consider. You may want to move or change the pictures from time to time, without upsetting the lighting pattern. A fixture such as a wallwasher attached to the ceiling or behind a molding or valance will flood the wall with light. Alternatively, use a row of downlights or uplights across the ceiling or floor or a track of spotlights angled right across the display area, fitted to the ceiling.

If you are lighting display shelves, try strip lighting above the shelves, concealed behind a valance or molding. Miniature spotlights can be concealed among the shelves or they can be used singly or again mounted on a track above, below, or the the side, and focused to show off items on the shelves. Downlights and uplights can also be used successfully, and if you place the objects inside a glass-fronted cabinet, the downlights and uplights can be tailored to fit inside also. Rows of tiny bulbs can be fitted across the top and bottom, down the sides, or along the front edge of the shelves. Alternatively, these can be mounted on a miniature track, but take care not to use anything too clumsy.

Glass shelves, for example, need to be very carefully lit and are better illuminated from above with concealed lighting or below with uplighting.

Lighting plants and flower arrangements is also important if they are to create impact and blend in with a room scheme at night. Since flower arrangements are frequently changed, and plants do need moving around occasionally, the lighting must be flexible. One of the most effective ways of doing this is to stand the plants on a glass-topped table and light them from below with an uplight. This can create dramatic shadow effects on the walls and ceiling. If plants are large, conceal the lighting among them. Any of the more conventional lighting methods can also be used. Keep some portable, adjustable lighting fixtures for lighting special flower arrangements.

Ways with Windows

The window treatment in a room is an integral part of the interior decorating scheme. As with color, pattern, and texture, and the selection of fabric and other materials, the style of window treatment will be influenced by the architecture of the room and the mood and atmosphere you wish to create. It will also be affected by the type, size, and shape of the window itself. Large, opulent drapes, for example, with a bold swag and jabots coming down over lace panels or delicate blinds look just right in big, bold windows in a traditional setting where there is plenty of space. Neat little café curtains, or crisp gingham-checked curtains with ruffled edges and a fabric valance are suitable for small windows in a country-style setting. Streamlined blinds or open-weave sheers are more suited to a modern theme.

Scale is important too. Big, bold patterns, bright colors, and dramatic treatments look best on large windows or where there are several windows on one wall that can be unified by floor-to-ceiling and wall-to-wall curtains. On the other hand, a pattern that has been cut short at a small window will look odd. Check the pattern repeat (length from top to bottom) of any fabric you are buying and consider it in relation to the window and curtain drop. Plain fabrics with small patterns and less vibrant colors tend to work better at small windows.

When choosing fabrics and trimmings for a window, make sure they are fairly long-wearing. Fabrics need to be resistant to fading and shrinking and be able to stand up to strong sunlight and condensation.

The texture and type of fabric is important and must be considered in relation to the size and scale of the window and the style of the room design and furnishings. Satins, velvets, brocades, silks, and taffetas, for example, will suit an elegant and more traditional setting, where the window treatment is a major part of the wall area. Lace, ruffled drapes, and balloon curtains can give a bedroom a soft romantic atmosphere. Tweeds, gray flannel, heavily pleated Roman shades, or streamlined venetians can be effective in a study or living room.

APPROACHES TO WINDOWS

Combining window treatments can be practical and energy-saving. Pull-down or pleated shades or natural wood, venetian, or even insulated blinds can be combined with curtains, which can, in turn, be lined and interlined. This can prevent as much heat loss as double-glazed windows. Sometimes blinds are fitted close to the glass, and curtains simply act as softly textured drapes. They can be lace or an open-weave sheer fabric. Closing the blinds at night under the curtains then gives extra privacy.

Where daytime privacy is essential, softly draped sheer curtains, lace panels, café-style

The kind of window treatment you choose will be determined by the style in which you choose to decorate, the shape and size of your windows, and the amount of privacy you desire. In rooms where privacy is not an issue, window frames need only be decorated with a fanciful swag. Swags can be purchased cut and sewn to the window's dimensions or can be a piece of fabric draped at your discretion.

curtains, ruffled jardinières, or festooned sheer blinds can be combined successfully with heavier curtains. A pull-down shade fitted close to the glass, or wooden or louvered shutters can also work well.

As alternatives to light curtains, use two tiers of café curtains or a pull-down shade that pulls up from the bottom. Both will let light in through the top part of the window.

Style coordination comes naturally in such multilayer treatments. Plain curtains can be trimmed with a border or fringe to match the sheer drapes; light under-curtains can be edged with ribbon or trimmed with pleated floral frill to match the curtains. Pull-down shades can be coordinated with the wallpaper and combined with plain or patterned curtains.

Windows can be screened in different ways to give privacy and still let in the light. A panel of garden trellis, painted white or a soft pastel color and attached to a frame for ease of removal, can help to hide an ugly view. Combined with an interesting selection of houseplants—some trained to climb the trellis—the effect is extremely striking. Wrought-iron grilles can be used similarly and are good for security.

Glass shelves placed across the windowsill and used to display a collection of colored glass, small objects, or plants and herbs are another decorative treatment for a window with little or no view. You will need to choose hardy plants and double-glaze the exterior pane if this idea is to work effectively in colder weather. Try to illuminate the display at night with concealed lighting under a valance above the window, from uplights below the sill, or with spotlights.

Interior shutters made of wood are sometimes found in older homes and can be ordered in standard sizes or custom-made. Shutters may be expensive to put in initially, but they have strong advantages: They give an elegant but not too formal look to a room, are easy to care for, and last for a long time.

Where daytime privacy is essential, softly draped sheer or lace curtains can be combined successfully with heavier curtains, while shades or blinds can be rolled down under decorative curtains. Tiers of curtains or partial shutters let in light while partially screening the window.

Texture and type of fabric contribute to the room's style. Satins, velvets, and brocades suit a more traditional setting, while lace and sheer curtains give a romantic atmosphere. Tweeds, gray flannel, Roman shades, or venetian blinds are most effective in a contemporary room.

Blinds, drapes, and café-style curtains can all be hung close to the glass. (Shutters can be drawn across these at night, with perhaps an extra layer of floor-to-ceiling heavy drapes.) Louvered panels can be used to replace or simulate shutters and make a very attractive window treatment in their own right.

SELECTING THE RIGHT TREATMENT

It can sometimes be difficult to judge how a certain window treatment will look, and how effective it will be as part of a room design.

One way of assessing results is to make elevated plans of the walls with windows to scale. Sketch on various styles until you achieve the correct balance. Alternatively, use overlays made of tracing paper, tissue paper, or transparent acetate. If you find it difficult to make the plan to scale visually, you can make templates for valances, swags, or jabots, and other drapes from brown paper. Make these actual size and pin them to the top of the window frame to judge the effect. This will also help you to judge the depth of a valance and the proper length of curtains.

Apart from selecting the right fabric or other material and deciding on the correct style for the room, the choice of window

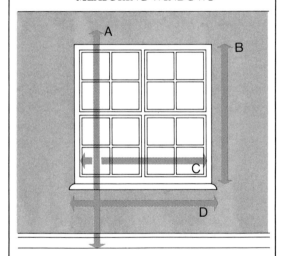

MEASURING WINDOWS

Windows must be measured accurately. Use a tape measure or ruler (fabric measures tend to stretch with use), and note down the measurements carefully.

Measure from the top of the window (or from the track or rod) to the floor (A) for floor-length curtains, or to the sill (B). If you are measuring for blinds or café curtains, measure the inside edge of the window frame (C). Measure the width of the window, or the length of the track or rod, if you intend to take the curtains past the edge of the frame (D).

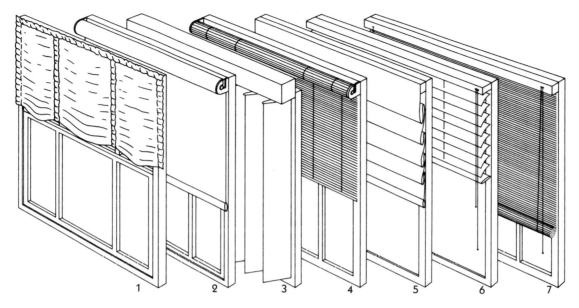

Blind lineup left to right: Festoon or Austrian sheers (1) are softly draped and drawn up with curtain-heading tape sewn vertically down the fabric at intervals. Sheer fabric is most suitable for this treatment. Pull-down shades (2) come in a wide range of colors and patterns in a stiffened fabric that is usually treated to shrug off dirt. If you make your own, choose a stiffish, smooth fabric that is not too bulky or textured. The roller has a retractable ratchet so the blind rolls up automatically. Vertical venetian blinds (3) come with different slat widths and in different-textured fabrics, metal, plastic, or wood. They can be designed to pull to left or right. Blinds (4) can be made from narrow strips of rattan and usually come in natural colors. Roman blinds (5) are a flat, pleated version of festoon blinds, and look neater and more tailored. Venetian blinds (6) come in different slat widths, including fine blinds that give a similar see-through effect to sheer curtains. Stunning effects can be created by mixing the slat colors to make striped and bordered blinds. Bamboo blinds (7) are similar to rattan blinds, but are more chunky and have the characteristic texture of bamboo.

treatment will also be determined by the type and actual shape of the window. In one house alone you may find a half dozen or more different styles of windows, and some of them may well present problems requiring knowledgeable decorating techniques.

WINDOW TYPES

Circular, or Palladian, windows   These became popular again in the 1980s, when neoclassical elements had such an influence on design, and they remain popular today. They are beautiful architectural elements, so if you move into a house that has them or are having new ones installed yourself, let them

show. Use a window treatment only for the straight square windows underneath them, hanging blinds or perhaps lace panels at the point where the curve of the arch begins. The treatment below will highlight the beauty of the windows above.

Attic windows or skylights   Often sloping, these windows may be difficult to treat neatly (nonprojecting dormers are different; see the following pages). Blinds can be fitted into new windows of this type, with the blinds sandwiched between two panes of glass to act as double glazing. Venetian blinds can be fitted, with a remote control, if the window or skylight is inaccessible. Shades can also be slotted into grooves parallel to the window

Look at the basic window shape and decide whether it should be enhanced and emphasized or disguised. Also consider the proportion: Look at the size and shape of the window in relation to the room and its position in the wall. You will also need to think about the window treatment style, which should echo the general furnishings and decorating theme and help to link the various surfaces with the furniture.

The window dressing, however simple, should never be treated as an afterthought or as an accessory—it should always be an integral part of your decorating plan. In fact, if patterned fabric is being selected for drapes, curtains, or blinds, it could well be the starting point for a color scheme.

Arched or Palladian windows

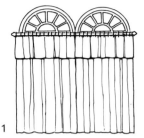

1

2

Arched or Palladian windows can be very beautiful. If screening is essential, try tiers of café curtains that leave the arched tops visible (1). If necessary, unify with full-length curtains under a valance (2).

Attic windows

3

4

Attic windows are either skylights or dormer windows. Skylights can be fitted with special venetian blinds (3) operated by remote control. For a softer look use curtains mounted on a rod (4), with a second rod at the angle of the slope.

frame with certain stop points, so that the shade can be adjusted. Insulated shades made especially for skylights are available to keep out the sun—and heat—on very hot days.

Bay and bow windows These can be square bay, angled bay, or bow (curved). Some are combined with deep windowsills or window seats, making long curtains impractical unless the window can be completely enclosed by them at night. Tracks following the line of the window can be concealed under a valance. Rods are another possible solution.

If a fitted window seat is to be used at night,

you can have floor-to-ceiling curtains on each side of the bay or bow and fitted blinds to the sill coordinated with the seat cushions. Alternatively, fit short curtains under the long ones. If the window needs screening for privacy during the day, combine long or short curtains with light curtains or blinds. The curtains can be café-style, and combined with a top tier or with long or short curtains. Crossover drapes also suit this type of window. In a contemporary setting, vertical blinds can be combined with curtains at the sides. If privacy is not a major issue, an alternative to curtains is a festooned treatment using a light fabric. This type of treatment will also soften the frame of the windows.

Bay or bow windows

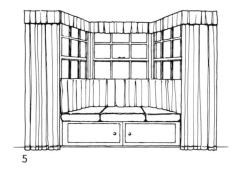

5

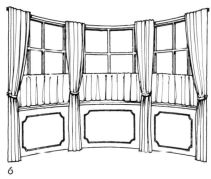

6

Bay windows can be squared off or angular; bow windows are usually gently curving. A window seat can be an attractive addition to an angular bay (5), with false curtains to each side of the window. The window can be partially screened with curtains. Full-length drapes, combined with short sheers, are a classic treatment for a bay (6).

Casement windows

7

8

Casement windows usually open outward. Choose either a small-scale pattern or plain fabric and keep the treatment neat. The window itself can be fitted with sheers, blinds, or café curtains, which swing in or out with the window (7). For a softer look have short, full curtains, under a frilled or pleated valance, that clear the window frame during the daytime (8).

Casement windows   In older homes, especially classic Tudors, casement windows may be small and fitted with leaded, diamond-shaped panes that tend to cut down on the light. They are unique to this type of architecture, and should be left untreated if possible.

Many contemporary homes may have casement windows that are much larger than the old-fashioned type. Houses built in the 1950s may also have casement windows that can be replaced by the new types, which are double-glazed. As with Tudor-style, the casements can be either double-sided (two windows together) or set singly in the wall. They can swing inward or outward.

If you want privacy or to keep out light, there are certain treatments that suit this type of window and conform to the room's design. With the type that swing in, the curtains must clear the window to enable it to be opened and closed. Short curtains that draw neatly to each side fitted under a valance work well, since the valance holds them away from the glass and frame. Curtains hung on a pole will also project into the room slightly. Café-style and shirred curtains and blinds can all be mounted on the actual window frame, a very practical treatment for windows that swing inward.

For casement windows that swing outward, window treatments can be placed on the larger window frame itself. This lets in maximum light, but softens the frame. Try a valance and drapes with tiebacks.

Dormer windows   Usually found in dormers in the roof of the house, these windows may be surrounded by both angled walls and ceilings in the interior of the house. Short curtains or blinds in almost any style look good if the dormer is a small one, and the space below the sill can often be filled with a built-in desk, dressing table, window seat, or suitable piece of furniture. For a more elegant treatment, hang floor-length, crossover drapes over a blind, or hang full-length curtains of soft fabric, held in place with tiebacks. Where dormer windows have Palladian-style tops, it may be necessary to combine one of these treatments with one suggested for Palladian-style windows.

French windows or doors   A soft treatment will make these look more elegant. If they are flanked by short windows on each side, they can be unified with shades or blinds—pull-downs, venetian, roman, or festooned—on the doors and to the sill on each window, combined with floor-to-ceiling and wall-to-wall heavy drapes. Alternatively, use vertical blinds (made of fabric) or vertical venetians (made of metal) right across the opening. Single or double French doors without side windows can be treated as tall windows or they can be fitted with drapes, blinds, or festoons fixed to the frame—unless you have a spectacular daytime view—and combined with curtains or vertical venetians. These treatments can also be adapted to front doors with side windows and to very large picture windows.

Narrow, tall windows   Narrow, tall windows seldom come in singles, except on a

Dormer windows

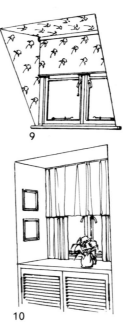

9

10

Dormer windows usually let in very little light. A simple pull-down shade (9) that retracts neatly during the daytime will let in maximum light. For a softer look, try tiers of café curtains, which can be made from a sheer fabric or lace (10). Crossover drapes can also look good in this situation.

French windows

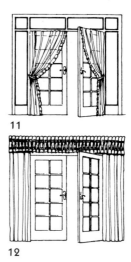

11

12

French windows are full-length versions of the casement window and usually open outward, but they can be used as internal, inward-opening doors. Double doors can be treated individually with drapes fitted to the frame (11), or crossover drapes can be used. A shirred valance looks attractive above French windows (12) with full-length curtains that pull to each side during the day.

landing or in a hall; it is more usual to find two or three on one wall. The best treatment is to unify them with full-length curtains that clear to each side of each window during the day, and form a continuous wall of fabric at night. If you want to make the windows appear shorter, choose fabric with a horizontal pattern, or make two or three tiers of café curtains. On one narrow window, take the track right past the frame, so that the curtains are fuller and also clear the frame during the day. Narrow, tall windows can also be combined on one wall with differently shaped windows,

Narrow, tall windows

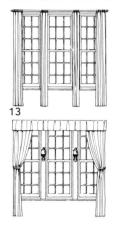

13

Double-hung or sash windows

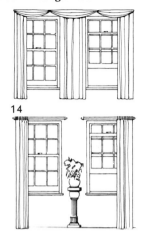

14

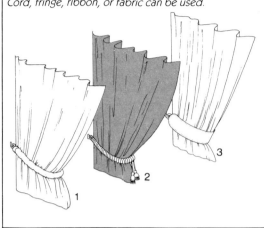

Tiebacks are used to hold the curtains in soft folds during the daytime, and can help to let in more light if they hold the curtains back clear of the frame. Cord, fringe, ribbon, or fabric can be used.

Narrow, tall windows can be made to seem shorter by combining full-length curtains to each side with short café curtains that come about halfway up the glass (13). A group of narrow, tall windows on one wall can be unified with a valance with curtains pulled to each side during the daytime. This works well if the windows are elegant, using the area of wall between the central windows to display pictures or **objets d'art** *(14).*

Double-hung or sash windows look best with an important elegant treatment. Combine full-length curtains with swags and jabots or valance (15). Two together on a wall can be treated as tall, narrow windows (16).

and, as with French doors, the secret of design success is to unify them.

Sash or double-hung windows Usually found in older homes, double-hung windows are still widely favored in newer ones as well. They slide open up and down and generally look best with a bold, elegant treatment, especially if they are part of a distinctive period-style setting. Opulent drapes in heavy fabrics with impressive valances, swags or festoons and jabots to top them will have this effect, or you can use curtains with pleats or other dra-

matic effects suspended on rods. Floor-length curtains suit sash windows and if combined with another treatment, the inner layer can be floor-length or just to the sill. Where two sash windows appear on one wall they can be dressed in a unified way, or you can attract attention to the space in between by making curtains on the two windows that pull to the edge of each frame. Place a picture, mirror, or other decorative item on the wall between the two windows, or some house-plants on a stand.

Patio doors and picture windows These are usually large, often a whole wall of window, and patio doors slide open or open out. Picture windows are not necessarily floor-length, but often run from wall to wall in a room, letting in the view. Patio doors are the modern equivalent of French doors and can be treated in a similar way. They usually let in so much light and sun it is essential to have treatments that really block these out when you want them to. Pleated, solar filter blinds that are transparent and diffuse light, cutting

Patio doors

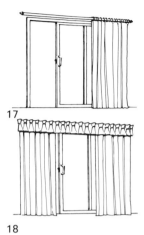

Patio doors often slide within their frames. Use floor-to-ceiling drapes and pull the curtains to one side for easy access (17). For a more formal room, use valance and full-length drapes to each side (18).

17

18

out harmful rays, are available. Curtains should be floor-to-ceiling length on both patio doors and picture windows, and from wall to wall. Pull them back to clear as much of the window as possible during the daytime and to avoid fading the fabric at the sides. Vertical blinds or shades are perfect for picture windows, since they allow you to let in as much or as little sun as you want.

For all curtain styles, floor-length curtains should just clear the floor for esthetics and protection of the curtains. Sill-length curtains should be exactly that, just to the sill and not hanging limply a few inches below. When the curtains have been washed or cleaned, the length may need adjusting. Allow for this when making curtains or having them made up.

DECORATING DIFFICULT WINDOWS

When faced with difficult windows, you can play tricks with window treatments that can deceive and please the eye.

- *Try to unify awkward corner windows* with the window treatment. (These usually come in pairs, on either side of a corner.) If the view is pleasant, hang curtains so that they pull back to the left and right, leaving all the glass clear. If the windows are tall, hang drapes or blinds down to the sill with full-length curtains on each side, unified at the top with a valance or festoon drapery. Café curtains look attractive when combined with a window seat, perhaps upholstered in a coordinated fabric.

  If the window has no view, pull-down shades with an interesting pattern or a painted "view" can be used and the window kept closed. If you need the window as a source of light, hang a blind that rolls up from the bottom, a sheer fabric blind, a lace panel, or sheer vertical blinds. Fine-slatted venetian blinds let in a surprising amount of light when slightly opened.

- *Make a narrow window look wider* by hanging curtains or draperies well over to each side of the frame—take the track or pole beyond the window edge.

- *Make a wide window look narrower* by keeping the curtains together at the top, and draped back softly at the sides with tiebacks.

- *Make a short window look taller* by placing the track well above the frame, and combining it with a focal point such as a canopy or pleated valance. Make the curtains floor-length or have several tiers of café curtains.

- *Make a small window look bigger* by hanging tiers of café curtains.

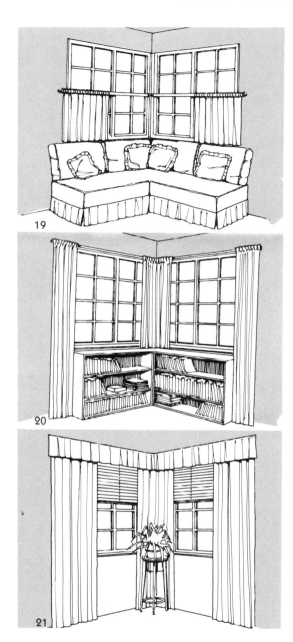

Awkward corner windows look better when unified. For an informal look, use café curtains on rods right into the corner—one or several tiers, depending on window height (19).

Furniture fitting into the corner (19, 20) can help link the two windows, but floor-length curtains to each side can be false, with shorter curtains to the sill providing the screen.

Blinds combined with full-length curtains will allow heat to circulate from radiators (21).

- *Make a tall window look shorter* by putting up a deep valance, preferably with an interesting shape, and hanging short curtains.

METHODS OF SUSPENSION

The style of curtain you select will determine the means of suspension and the type of heading or topping the curtains need.

If the curtains are to hang from a curtain rod, this will be mounted on brackets above the window frame. Pleated curtain headings can form a decorative part of the overall look. There are various ways of pleating headings (see pages 100–101), and rods can either be fitted with rings or have gliders concealed in the lower edges of the rod. The curtains can be headed with tape, and conventional hooks used to slip into the gliders or the special eyes in the rings.

Alternatively, round rings can be sewn to the back of each pleat in the curtain heading, and the rod can be passed through them. Pleated headings can also be combined with a sleek, neat curtain track that is designed to be seen.

If the curtains are to be fitted with valances at the top, they can have a simple, gathered heading since it won't be seen. Valances need a double rod, one part for the curtain to move along and the other part for the valance. Both curtains and valance are attached to the track by means of hooks, slipped through the heading, and passed through gliders on the track.

Café curtains are usually mounted on special rods, which are then fixed to the window frame or mounted on each side of it on brackets. The curtains can be headed in any of the conventional ways or they can be scalloped. Some café curtains have special casings through which the rod can pass. Neat, slim-line track, which is usually attached to the top of the window frame, will come complete with gliders. Hooks in the heading tape then fix the curtains to the track. Shirred curtains and some drapes are attached to the window frame by special extending wire, although they can also be attached by a narrow rod. The curtains either have a casing at the top, and sometimes bottom edge as well, or the wire or rod is slipped through a hem. Sheers can also be headed like conventional curtains—although special "invisible" heading tape needs to be used—and then pleated or gathered. They can be suspended by means of poles or track.

Curtain panels may cover the entire window or be made to café-curtain length and require two hems top and bottom that take either wooden or brass poles. The top pole is attached by hooks at either side while the bottom pole hangs free to keep the panel uniformly flat.

Commercially made curtain panels have their own means of mounting and suspension and may be electrically operated to slide open or closed.

Tracks and poles are also available for special treatments. If you put a curtain behind a door, for example, in order to prevent its catching each time the door is opened or closed you will need a special portière rod that rises and falls as the door opens. Curtains for dividers can be attached to the ceiling by means of ceiling-mounted track, sometimes actually embedded in the ceiling, poles, cubicle curtain track, or rods. All blinds come complete with their own means of mounting and suspension.

Pinch pleats gather up the fabric crisply and look decorative (1). Pencil pleats form neat, regular folds and need a lot more fabric, about three times the track width (2). Triple pinch pleats give a fuller curtain than single or double pleats but allow a softer drape than pencil pleating (3). Tops can be scalloped or lace/sheers clipped into rings on a rod (4).

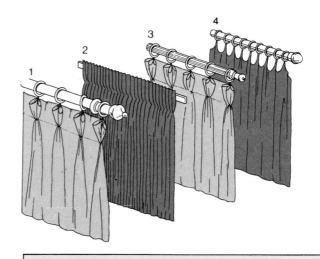

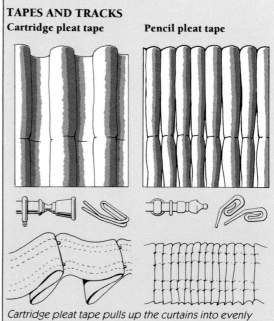

TAPES AND TRACKS

Cartridge pleat tape   **Pencil pleat tape**

Cartridge pleat tape pulls up the curtains into evenly spaced, rounded cartridge pleats. It is particularly good with heavyweight fabrics such as velvets and brocades.

Pencil pleat tape pulls up the fabric to form even pencil pleats. This tape can be used on all fabric weights and comes in a variety of widths. Between two and a quarter and two and a half times the track length of fabric is needed for this tape.

Softly gathered valance, combined with curtains with
tiebacks (1). Box-shape valance, which is usually
preformed, can be covered with either fabric or
wallpaper to match the scheme or painted (2). Shaped
valance is usually made from fabric stiffened with
buckram (3). Drapable fabric and sheers can be softly
gathered to form a fall of fabric at the side of the frame
(4).

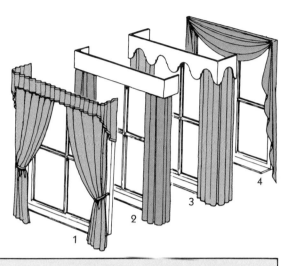

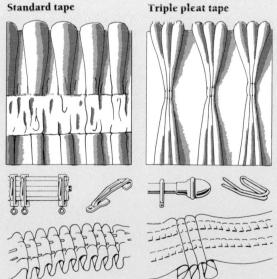

Standard tape

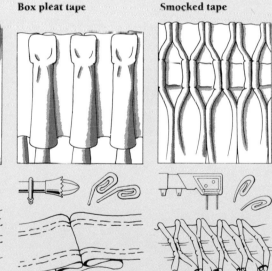

Triple pleat tape

Box pleat tape

Smocked tape

Standard tape is the simplest and cheapest form of
heading tape. It merely gathers the fabric. Use it under
valances or in kitchens and bathrooms. It looks best with
lightweight, unlined curtains.

Triple pleat tape. When stitching this tape, work from
where the curtains will meet outward so that the groups
of pleats are evenly spaced and the curtain tops match
across each curtain.

When box pleat tape is pulled up, the curtain top folds
into evenly spaced box pleats. Because of the pleat
widths, this works well with heavier, lined curtains. You
will need roughly two and a half times the track length
of fabric.

Smocked tape is one of the range of decorative heading
tapes, which cleverly gives the fabric top a smocked
effect. It is most suited to sheer fabrics but can be used
on most other curtaining fabrics.

DESIGN RENEWAL

YOUR INTERIOR DESIGN PROBLEM MAY NOT REQUIRE a complete scheme change, it may simply be a matter of minor alteration. Ugly pipes, an unattractive fireplace, a dull or dark color scheme, or garish bathroom tiles are all minor problems, but they can spoil the overall look of a room.

Different solutions designed to suit different styles are described and illustrated in this trouble-shooting section. A room can sometimes just feel wrong for no apparent reason. Flipping through this section may help you identify the cause of the problem as well as show you how to rectify it with a minimum of fuss. Even if your particular problem is not included here, you will probably find a solution to it among the wealth of suggestions for concealing, disguising, and enhancing different features.

Renovation may not be something you would consider undertaking yourself, but it is useful to know what will be involved in, for example, repairing plasterwork. Experts may suggest more drastic renovation than is absolutely necessary, and this section outlines the alternatives. It also looks at problem structural surfaces that may have to be dealt with before redecoration is started. Ways of disguising poor ceilings and walls, leveling uneven floors, choosing doors, and renovating decrepit staircases are all suggested.

The section on camouflage deals with problems of proportion. Simple visual illusions can transform a room with color and pattern—making a high room seem lower, blending projections and recesses into the background, or even creating interest in a boring, box-shaped room.

Solving Built-in Problems

When you look at your home with a view to decorating it or reworking an existing plan, you will probably find that its attractive features are offset by other, less pleasing, characteristics. Some houses or apartments are just badly designed. Others simply have minor irritations such as three windows of different shapes on one wall, unattractive though practical built-in furniture, and dark corridors, halls, and landings that are sometimes cluttered with pipes and cables. All these problems can be dealt with and some of the solutions are surprisingly simple.

If you have recently moved to a new home, you may find it difficult to fit in your existing furniture, curtains, carpets, and accessories so that they blend with the new environment and the existing decor. There are also mistakes you may have made yourself when decorating. A wall covering, flooring, or upholstery fabric that looked superb in the shop may just not work when it is up on your wall or down on your floor. Cabinetry and work surfaces can also cause problems—they often do not look the same in reality as they did in the catalog or shop. Or, once you have completed your decorating scheme, you may find that you are left with a garish or boring room.

If such disheartening problems arise, look at the room or particular difficulty as critically and clinically as possible. It may help to pretend that you are not dealing with your own home but rather with a situation you are trying to solve professionally. If this proves difficult, ask a neighbor, friend, or member of the family for an unbiased opinion. You may be surprised at how quickly the right solution springs to mind, or indeed how many possible solutions there are.

PIPES

You certainly cannot dispense with the plumbing, but visible pipes can be an eyesore. They are most likely to occur in older homes where thoughtless replanning, replumbing, or conversion work has gone on over the years. Basement corridors and hall or landing areas are particularly prone to these problems. Kitchens and bathrooms can also suffer from the presence of too many pipes.

Solving the Problem

A very simple solution You might apply wallpaper over the pipes, using paper with a striking pattern. The pipes are then hardly noticeable. Alternatively, you can leave some exposed and paint the rest to match the overall color of the wallpaper or use paint techniques such as spattering, marbling, or sponging. These work particularly well if the walls and baseboards are treated similarly. You might wish to make a feature of the pipes by painting them in strong, contrasting, primary colors. For a more traditional look, paper behind the pipes with a busy pattern, and paint the pipes in one or more of the colors in the paper.

Boxing in the pipes   This is another option, so long as you have accessibility to them. Boxing-in is practical and can be made almost invisible if you paint the box to match the wall or baseboards or by using a little trompe l'oeil. You can also make the box match the cabinetry in a room. Overlapping one side of a corner box makes an alcove for small shelves. If you back the shelf with mirror tiles, the illusion is created that the shelves run from the front to the back of the wall. For horizontal pipework, you can make a planter, sizing the box so that it is large enough for standard plant pots. The boxwork can then be painted.

RADIATORS

Central heating is normally used in cold climates, but the sources of heat vary from house to house. Conventional or old-fashioned upright radiators are likely, at best, to be noticeable or, at worst, to dominate the whole room. Their location in the room can be wrong, too—many radiators, for example, are placed under the main window, causing a great deal of heat loss. In some rooms this positioning makes fitting in the furniture difficult, especially where the ideal place for a desk, work or play surface, dressing table, bath, sink, window seat, or indoor plants would be under the window.

Solving the Problem

Treat the radiator decoratively   It can fade into the background. Either paint it to match

Boxing in a space-hogging radiator can give it another function. Incorporate it into the design scheme, for example. In this nursery the radiator is encased in a wooden box that has been cut into the shape of a picket fence. In a few months, when the room's occupant is crawling and toddling around, the radiator cover will keep him or her safely away from a necessary source of heat.

the surrounding wall area or paint it to match the background of the wall covering behind it. You can also incorporate the radiator in an integral, striking design. Paint the wall with an interesting pattern—trompe l'oeil clouds or contemporary graphics—and continue the design on to the surface of the radiator.

Make a feature of the radiator   In the right situation, such as a child's room, playroom, or game room, you can give it a flamboyant treatment so that it really stands out. It can be painted in bold colors to look like a flag, decorated to look like a sheep, zebra, tiger, or other favorite animal, or made to look like a train, car, or ship, if the room has a definite theme of that kind. You can make it thoroughly decorative with garlands of flowers.

Replace the existing radiator   Find a more attractive model. Facsimiles of old-fashioned designs that stand on the floor against the wall are available. There are other individual

The owners of this house wanted a library, so they converted the dining room and lined the walls with bookshelves. Many of the bookshelves were built around existing radiators that were covered in wood to create window seats. Some window seats do not cover radiators, and these have panels concealing space for storage. Window seats that do cover radiators have grills to allow the heat to circulate.

designs of elegant shape and finish, with basic styles sufficiently adaptable to fit comfortably into a variety of schemes for decor and furnishing. Alternatively, there are now some contemporary designs that look almost like wall sculptures, available in a vast range of colors for a more contemporary appearance.

Box in a radiator   For an elegant room, use a grille of brass or another metal so that the heat can still circulate, or conceal the radiator with a wooden grid or trellis, either natural or painted, to suit the chosen scheme. In the right situation, in a bow or bay window or where there is a deep reveal, you can combine this treatment with a window seat.

Blend in the radiator   This will work if it comes under a windowsill and there is space at each side of the window. Have vertical venetian blinds made, with a space cut out in the middle. This cutout is made by combining short and long slats—the long slats coming to either side of the window frame, and the short ones to the sill.

If the window is very attractive and the radiator is not very high, the window dressing can be a problem. Where you do not need curtains, paint the window frame and the radiator in a strong color, and treat the window with a decorative pull-down shade that can be bought ready-made or ordered to your own design.

Divert attention from the radiator   Position a shelf along the top, mounted on brackets clear of the top of the radiator. Here you can display an eye-catching collection of objects or plants. Again, paint the shelf and radiator to match the basic wall color. Take this idea a step further and use the whole wall area for a complete run of shelves, incorporating the radiator.

If several radiators are positioned on a long wall, paint them to match the background. Hang large pictures framed to the same size as the radiators above each one and light with a spotlight.

FIREPLACES

Fireplaces are a popular feature in most homes. But in older houses and apartments, you may find that the fireplace and surround (mantel and brick or stone area around the opening) are not in working or pristine condition or may simply be ugly. There are various ways of converting a fireplace either to make it into an attractive focal point or to make it unobtrusive so that it blends in with the room. Taking out a fireplace is a possibility, but that can be heavy work.

Solving the Problem

Enhance the surround   Paint it to contrast with the wall area or use a painting technique such as marbling, stippling, or rag rolling. A good-looking wood mantelpiece may have had countless layers of paint applied over the decades and stripping the paint and waxing the wood will transform it. You may even find when you strip the surface that the surround is made of marble and not wood. Test a small area on the underside of the mantelpiece, because some wood strippers are not suitable for use on marble and will damage the surface.

Convert the fireplace   Place a wood stove within the fireplace opening. There is a wider range than ever of styles of wood stoves to match any decor.

Disguise the surround   If it is not particularly interesting but you do not want to remove it, decorate the surround to match the background, so that the fireplace merges into the wall. Make an eye-catching arrangement in the recessed spaces by installing shelves, perhaps above low cupboards, with arched alcoves. Hang a bold picture, wall-hanging, or other focal point on the wall above the fireplace.

Convert the interior part   Leave the fireplace surround intact and use the interior for another purpose. It can make an attractive alcove to house a television set or stereo equipment, or it can become a small built-in cupboard or an open bookcase.

If you want to make a dramatic focal point of the area, put concealed lighting into the recess, back it with a mirror, and display a collection of plants, a flower arrangement, or china or glass objects. Glass shelves could also be installed across the recess and small, decorative items displayed.

Rearrange the furniture You can simply conceal the fireplace. In a bedroom, for example, the bed can be placed against the mantelpiece, and the fireplace surround might act as a headboard. The mantel might be incorporated into a dressing-table design. In a dining area, storage units or freestanding furniture of different depths can be selected, some filling the recesses, the narrower ones butting up to the mantel, and all fitting flush at the front. In a sitting area, a sofa can conceal an unsightly fireplace. A folding screen of wood or painted panels can provide a good temporary disguise, or even a long wall-hanging or rug can do the trick.

DARK ROOMS

Dark ground-floor rooms need a light touch. Sometimes when two rooms are combined into one, one end can seem dark and dismal. Or when an extension is added, it can reduce the light from one or more rooms. Rapidly growing trees and hedges, projecting fences or walls, and tall buildings can all create a similar problem in a room.

Solving the Problem

Use a mirror The reflected light will help brighten the room. Test the mirror's position until you find the point where there is maximum reflection. In rooms with recessed walls, a mirror can be positioned on the back wall of an alcove. Illuminate with concealed lighting or attractive uplights for maximum nighttime effect.

Decorate the room in sunshine colors Bright clear yellow and sparkling white create an illusion of light, or use sunset colors of orange, flame, and gold with white.

Install glass panels in doors If this see-through look will interfere with privacy, put mirrors into the door panels instead or use frosted, colored, or patterned glass.

Remove heavy curtains If a window or back door at the dark end of the room has heavy curtains that shut out light, replace them with floor-to-ceiling lace drapes, which can create an impression of light, and install a pull-down shade behind the drapes to create privacy when the room is lit at night.

Alternatively, use a row of vertical venetian blinds. They are available in a range of bright colors as well as metallic finishes and let in a great deal of light when partially opened, at the same time ensuring privacy.

Make attractive lighted displays Indoor plants, objects grouped on a glass-topped table, ornaments or sculpture, or a well-displayed picture can be illuminated with uplights, spotlights, or, in the case of pictures, picture gallery lighting.

BUILT-IN FURNITURE

Built-in cabinets, furniture, and closets are often convenient, but they may be too bulky or obvious for the style of your rooms. However, built-in furniture can be dressed up to look elegant or tempered so that it merges with the surroundings. Treat the furniture in

To make this nursery seem larger, the cabinetry needed to store baby's supplies and clothes was built into the wall. Almost everything in the room was painted white, and the furnishings were upholstered in pale colors to make the space seem larger and airier. To keep that pale scheme from being monotonous, the cabinet shelves are painted the blue-green found in the fabric, and blue-green ducks are stenciled on the door.

different ways, according to the decor and function of each room. Look for potential in old, well-constructed items of furniture, but don't waste time and money on poorly made pieces. Cheap veneered surfaces cannot be improved even by painting, but you may be lucky and find beautiful solid wood underneath layers of old paint.

Solving the Problem

Paper the cabinet or closet fronts Coordinate these with the wall coverings and fabrics used in the room. Most wall coverings adhere easily to a cupboard door but can curl up at the edges with constant handling. Take a paper or vinyl wall covering to within 1 inch of the edge of the door or drawer and hide the raw edges under decorative molding, glued into position.

Take the doors off altogether Replace them with colorful pull-down shades for a lighter look, or light and lacy fabric curtains.

Paint the whole unit Use a fairly strong color to match the rest of the decor. Paint or stain the panels and place plain wooden edging around them in a contrasting color. Attach a simple wooden garden trellis with a diamond pattern to form panels on a plain area. Change handles or knobs to suit the new style.

Use special painting techniques You can enliven the surface finish. Get out a paintbrush or some sponges and rags, paint, and glaze, and start experimenting with marbling, sponging, stippling, dragging, rag rolling, combing, or scumbling (simulating a highly decorative wood grain). These paint techniques create a feeling of space and translucency and amazing effects can be achieved. Free brochures from paint manufacturers telling how to work with these techniques are available in hardware stores.

Cans of spray paint are available in a wide range of colors, and even faux finishes such as marbling can come out of a can of spray paint. They are easy to handle when painting small areas such as doors and drawer fronts.

To avoid smudges, runs, and sags in the paint while you are working on doors, it is often best to take them off their hinges and lay them flat. Always take drawers out of furniture and work on them horizontally.

Use a stenciled design It is possible to create an entirely new personality for furniture used as storage units. Strip off the old surface if necessary, clean thoroughly, and repaint. Stencil with traditional border patterns, such as a Greek-key or a simple flowering vine design. There are many border papers in these styles that you can use as templates for cutting stencils—or use the borders themselves. Alternatively, plan a Delft-tile look in blue and white, or an Etruscan effect with black and terra-cotta.

Paint a pattern Start on the doors, drawers, top, and sides of the furniture, and carry the pattern over onto the wall behind and above or add touches that echo the design. You can use any of the ideas suggested previously for radiators, or invent your own. Try a leafy tree or cloudy sky motif in a small, square room to add an extra dimension.

ROOMS WITH NO VIEW

When you choose a home, you doubtless pay particular attention to the natural light coming into the main living areas and the view from the windows. But there may be some internal rooms, such as the bathroom and inner hall, that have no windows at all. The main rooms may also have a bleak view, such as a window that looks out onto a wall. Some windows can look into neighboring houses, and windows high up in the recesses to each side of a fireplace may let in some light but be unattractive.

Solving the Problem

Take out the old glass Replace it with stained glass in a design and style to suit the house, its furnishings, and the overall decor. There are stained-glass artists who will do custom designs, but you can also find old stained-glass panels in antique shops and from merchants who sell architectural artifacts taken from old buildings. Special leading materials are available if you want to install the panels yourself.

Display a collection of colored glass against the window   This is another interesting way of getting colorful light filtering through. Even simple, crudely designed bottles will do. Place shelving across the window to hold the collection—adjustable brackets are the most practical means of suspension.

Use soft furnishings imaginatively   A beautiful lace panel, filmy drape, or sheer woven fabric can act as an attractive screen. Combine the fabrics with a blind hung close to the glass for nighttime privacy. A filmy festoon can also act as a fabric screen under heavier drapes (see pages 89–101 for more ideas).

Close off an ugly window with screens   These can be made of rattan, wrought iron, or other metals. Extremely effective screens can be made from a simple garden trellis mounted on a frame that fits the window opening exactly. It looks particularly effective when houseplants are trained to climb or to trail over it.

Plain Walls

A large expanse of blank wall can look stark and cold, especially above the sofa in the living room or the headboard in the bedroom. It can also be dull across from a row of cupboards in a bedroom or at the side of the stairs.

A textured or patterned wall covering may not be the correct answer to the problem, since there may already be several other patterned surfaces in the room. One obvious

treatment is to pattern with solids—that is, arrange groups of objects or pictures to produce an impression of a pattern on the surface.

Attach fabric to the wall   You can cover up the unwanted surface in several ways. Paper-backed fabrics can be pasted on but may be difficult to remove and tricky to keep clean. For ordinary fabrics, battens can be fixed around the perimeter of the wall and, if necessary, across the wall area. The fabric is then stretched and pinned over the battens, and can be taken down for cleaning. Staple guns are also used for fixing fabric, particularly for a pleated effect. Also, special fabric tracks are available that are placed at the top, bottom, and sides of the wall. The fabric is tucked behind the track with a special tool.

Fabric may also be hung on a curtain track at the top of the wall; it can then flow free or be pinned at the baseboards. Curtain wires at the top and bottom will give a very attractive shirred effect.

Commission a mural or trompe l'oeil design   Some trompe l'oeil looks so real that a painted garden scene outside a painted window does fool the eye at first sight. The perspective in the painting gives added dimension to the room, making it appear larger than it is.

Separate walls horizontally   On a tall rather than long blank wall area, create a chair rail and decorate differently above and below it. Divide the wall horizontally, about 3–3½ feet up, parallel with the baseboards, with plaster molding, or substitute molding made of rigid foam that looks just like the real thing when painted. Treat the lower and upper areas of the wall in different ways.

Paper one section and paint the other. Use companion or coordinating papers. Hang a heavy wall covering on the lower half, or put in wood paneling. Attach a trellis to either section of the wall, painted to contrast with the background, and set it off in the other section with a floral-and-trellis pattern on paper. This treatment works particularly well in tall halls and long corridors. Paint a trellis or grid pattern to simulate the look of trellis, adding shadows to enhance the illusion.

PASSAGES AND HALLWAYS

Large houses and apartments may have spacious, well-lit individual rooms, but narrow, gloomy passages and stairwells. To worsen the impression, inner passages are frequently peppered with doorways, often breaking up the wall area in awkward places.

You can create a light and airy effect with the right choice of color scheme and clever decorations. You may be able to let in some natural daylight, or trap some reflected light, but you may have to face the fact that some form of artificial light will be necessary most of the time.

Solving the Problem

Create a terraced effect   Choose the longest unbroken wall and decorate with a mural, possibly seen through a colonnade if you like a classical style. Marble all the woodwork to echo the pillars and use trees in pots and indoor plants if there is room and light. If not,

Dimly lit halls can be brightened up in several ways. Light is provided by fluorescent tubes, concealed behind moldings (1). The light bounces off the ceiling, bringing warmth and a diffused glow to the area. The original door in this hall is given the Gothic treatment (2). A lighting frame is constructed from ceiling panels and used to hide light fittings (3). A fanlight is installed above the door to let in some natural light without losing any privacy (4). Display fittings are built to each side of the front door and include concealed lighting to illuminate the whole area (5). An inner porch is created from glass bricks, softly diffusing light through the hall (6).

paint the plants on the wall to enhance the patio image further. Alternative trompe l'oeil effects include a blue sky with puffy white clouds, a green garden, a bright view of spring saplings, or absolutely any scene you would like to live with. If the corridor ends in a door, try treating the wall and door at the end in a similar way. Paint a view seen through the door so that it looks as though it is permanently open onto a vista.

Bright, sunshine colors   Papering the walls with a pretty pattern on a light background is a simple solution. Echo the background of the paper for most of the woodwork, but paint all the doors a clear, bright color. If the paper is multicolored, you might choose a different hue for each door or paint the ceiling a pale, clear, sky blue.

Create a window   On a blank wall, create your window using a frame, mirror glass, or mirror tiles. Light the area carefully to create a subdued reflected glow.

DULL COLOR SCHEMES

A carefully planned scheme worked around neutral or very pale colors or a monochromatic decor can look dull and flat. Despite a perfect paint finish, it can seem to lack personality. Injecting more life into a dull room does not necessarily involve redecorating or refurnishing. First establish why the colors have not worked or what is still missing.

Solving the Problem

Create some bright focal points   Often a room looks dull because it lacks accents and accessories or has insufficient color contrast. Try a few bright cushions scattered on the sofas and chairs or a colorful hand-woven throw, a collection of colored glass in an attractive display, some pretty ornaments, or a well-planned group of pictures and prints, an exotic sculpture, or a large piece of unusual pottery.

Break up the surface textures   If textures are too similar or there is not enough balance between patterned and plain surfaces, make some changes. Add shiny textures to a room with mainly matte finishes, harsh ones to an overly soft look and matte surfaces to an overly shiny scheme.

Change the lighting   You can bring a room to life by introducing some pools of light from lamps, possibly with lamp shades in pale, subdued colors. Try spotlighting some areas or putting concealed lighting behind a valance or molding. Place a decorative rug under a glass table. Don't underestimate the power of houseplants to brighten a room.

Rearrange the furniture   The positioning of furniture may add to a dull effect, as when pieces are squarely placed with backs parallel to the wall. A sofa can go at right angles to a wall facing another sofa or two chairs, with a coffee table in between to make an inviting conversation area. In a living-dining room try a similar grouping and back the sofa with a serving table or sideboard, making a natural division between the two parts of the room. In a bedroom move the headboard away from the wall and suspend fabric from the ceiling to divide the spaces. Alternatively, position wardrobes behind the bed, so they open the other way and act as a more solid room divider. That way you will have a separate dressing area and a cozy, intimate sleeping area. Make a scale plan with cutouts of the furniture shapes (see pages 10–11) to make sure everything will fit in before you move heavy pieces.

Use a cover-up technique Change the color of the walls: paint over paper, hang a patterned wall covering, or drape the walls with fabric. Break up the overall plainness of large floor areas with one or more rugs. Use patterns with solids.

Alter the window treatment A venetian blind under curtains can add interest if the two contrast with each other, as do some heavy drapes with flamboyant ties and a valance over simple blinds.

SOFT FURNISHINGS

When you move into a new home, your drapes may not fit the existing windows. If they are made from good quality fabric, perhaps lined and interlined, you may not want to change them. It is possible to make curtains "stretch" to fit, although in some cases it is more sensible to cut them down to fit a smaller window or to make them into table covers, cushions, lampshades, and other accessories.

Existing upholstery can also be a problem in a new environment, especially if you have left your curtains and carpets behind in the old house and either kept the ones in your new home from the previous occupant or purchased new ones. There are several ways of making these soft furnishings fit into your new scheme.

Solving the Problem

Lengthen curtains and drapes If the tops are simple or pleated with tape, add extra fabric to them to make them the right length. Cover up the seam with a dramatic valance or swags and jabots at the top of the curtain in a contrasting or complementary fabric.

Trim curtain hems with fringe and braid This works if the curtains are a few inches short. Or you can add bands of contrasting fabric or color. If you decide to add a decorative border, you can carry it up the sides of the curtains and across a valance. Echo the effect in a wallpaper frieze or painted border so it looks like part of the design theme.

Widen narrow curtains A border trim at each side will make curtains wider. If the curtains are pinch-pleated, change the pleating tape for a less tightly gathered one to gain extra width. If this still does not bridge the gap, buy a contrasting fabric and add wide bands to the outside edges of the curtains. You can contrast patterns with solids and vice versa. You can also make striped curtains—take out the seams and let in widths of different fabric—or split widths for a narrower stripe. Aim for an integrated look, using the contrasting fabric for a dramatic top treatment to the curtains.

Use color to integrate soft furnishings Blend them together with new furnishings by changing their color. If the color is wrong but the curtains fit, you may be able to dye them yourself. (Get expert advice before starting.) If the fabric is good and the curtains are lined and interlined, have them professionally dyed. You may find that the fabric is not suitable for dyeing for one of several reasons. Some fabrics, particularly some synthetics, will not dye well. Some fabrics will shrink. In some cases, the dye can cause the fabric to rot. It is not usually possible to dye from dark to light. Color can be completely stripped out of some fabrics, but this process badly weakens the fibers—faded curtains may actually shred if color-stripped. You cannot obliterate pattern with dye, but you do get an interesting textured effect with some designs when you dye them.

Upholstery can sometimes be dyed in the home; there are also professional firms who will take the furniture away for recoloring. Be guided by the experts and do not be surprised if the finished result does not look quite as you expected. It may be better to consider a different approach and use new, loose, or tailored covers. As a temporary measure you can make a throw cover. Try a lace panel or delicate shawl on a bedroom chair or sofa, or use an attractive blanket, rug, or quilt on a leather or tweed cover. You can make a quick throw-and-tie cover from bed sheets, which come in a huge and highly designed range today. Sometimes a vast collection of different-shaped and colored cushions thrown in profusion onto a sofa or chair will be so striking that you do not need to recover the item at all.

WOODWORK

It can be surprisingly difficult to find the right woodwork treatment for a room. The one you select may not work, but this may not be apparent until the entire scheme is complete. Yet sometimes it is a pity to play safe with neutral-toned doors, baseboards, and window frames and sills and just go for the easy option by painting them to match the background wall covering, fabric, or carpet.

Painting woodwork white is also a mistake if there are off-white items in the room, such as built-in furniture, cabinets or carpets. A brilliant white woodwork will make them look dirty unless the walls are also white. If you plan to use a neutral tone, color-match it carefully to an existing item or background.

Solving the Problem

Create an interesting texture   Use one of the special painting techniques, such as marbling, rag rolling, dragging or sponging, or stippling. You can brighten or deepen the color using one of these techniques. Take care to choose the right color value to put on top of the existing one. Test the effect on a separate piece of paper or a card when you are trying one of these attractive texturing methods.

Try stripping the wood   The warm look of polished wood can transform a room. Take all the existing paint off the woodwork, right down to the natural wood. Clean and then wax or seal the surface. Most available paint strippers allow you to work on a small area at a time. Doors can be difficult to strip, particularly if they have moldings and panels, and it may be easier and more convenient to have them stripped professionally.

Color-stain or stencil natural woodwork   Stenciling on a bright pattern is an alternative to plainly stripped woodwork. Or you can paint door moldings or panels in a contrasting color or a lighter or darker shade of the original color.

KITCHEN AND BATHROOM FIXTURES

It can be irritating, when you move into a home with a well-equipped kitchen or bathroom, not to like the color or style of the cabinets and appliances, the finish and design of the work counters, the pattern on the ceramic tiles, or the color of the bathroom fixtures. There are, however, ways to give cabinets and tiles a face-lift that will allow you to modify the design without having to replace the units.

Solving the Problem

Replace cabinet doors and drawer fronts
Some manufacturers supply spare sections for their cabinets, so find out who made yours and whether different colors or designs are available. There are also specialist companies that will make new doors to order, but it is only worthwhile changing the doors if the units are of very good quality, and are strong and sound. Unfinished wooden cabinet doors of different sizes are also available from large home improvement stores.

Cover cabinet doors and drawer fronts
For a country look, use thin tongue-and-groove wood paneling. Before you do, however, make sure that the additional weight is not too great for the existing hinges and frames; otherwise, the doors might warp or drop slightly, making opening and closing them difficult.

Set the tongue-and-groove on a diagonal rather than a vertical. Or try a horizontal pattern, which gives a more solid impression than a vertical pattern. Painting the tongue-and-groove in a shiny or satin finish or colored wood stain will eliminate a rustic look where a contemporary one would work better. Alternatively, you can antique the timber and seal it in a matte finish to get a traditional look.

Brighten kitchen units Use any of the methods for built-in furniture (see pages 109–11). Note that laminated and plastic surfaces cannot be painted but can be sprayed with certain paint treatments. All surfaces except for the work surfaces can be colored in this way. If you have cabinets made of wood, try a dragged paintwork look using washable paint in pastel colors. The effects can be quite stunning.

Give cabinets and drawers a minor facelift
Simply change handles or knobs and add beading or narrow molding. Bright-colored plastic handles can look extremely good in a contemporary kitchen.

Change or cover work surfaces Some laminates can have a new layer bonded on top. Thick tiles can be used for work surfaces and can sometimes be applied to an existing surface, but they may need a frame or heavy-duty underpinning. Quarry tiles are a good choice. Special tile kits, complete with edging tiles, are available and are fairly easy to handle. Be sure to use the correct type of tile grouting, one that is impervious to cooking liquids and acids. Choose a contrasting grout color for a more striking effect.

Cover up existing wall tiles If you cannot live with the color or pattern of the old tiles, you can retile on top of them. If the existing tiles have a heavy "nosing" (ridge of tiles) around the top, remove this carefully. Neaten the edge with a wood batten after retiling.

Cover old tiles with a laminate, either bonded to the new tiles or stuck to a baseboard, which is then attached to the wall, or with thin strips of wood.

STORAGE SPACE

Adequate storage space is often lacking in contemporary homes. With a little thought,

Ceramic tiles come in all shapes, sizes, colors, and textures. Look for interesting border designs and tiles, ridged and marbled textures. Always use a floor-grade tile for flooring, not a wall-grade one. Floor tiles can be made from different materials—cork, carpet, linoleum, vinyl, marble, or ceramic. Make sure you get the right type for the particular job you have in mind. Floor tiles are not easy to handle, especially in small, cramped spaces, where intricate cutting is required.

furnishings can be planned to include either temporary or permanent storage.

Solving the Problem

Use corrugated plastic stacking boxes These boxes, or bright and cheerful racks available at office supply stores, can store children's clothes, toys, or tools. Store very small items in wire letter trays.

Double up Storage space can also provide a table or work surface. Old trunks, wicker chests, or blanket chests can be used in this way. For long-term storage, use the trunk or chest as a bedside table or position it at the end of the bed. Castors fixed to the bottom of a heavy trunk or box make it much easier to move.

Use a bentwood hat stand It makes a decorative bathroom or bedroom stand on which to hang towels and bathrobes. If you have a plain one, either strip it and apply polyurethane, or decorate it with one of the paint techniques, such as speckling, to match your overall color scheme.

Renovation and Camouflage

No place is perfect; most homes have one or two drawbacks. These problems may be the result of a previous owner's mistake or your own. It could be an actual built-in design fault such as an awkwardly shaped room, or a room that is too dark or too bright, or one that is proving impossible to furnish successfully, no matter how many times you change the plan. A room can be too tall, or have a low or sloping ceiling. It can also be too narrow or boxlike, too dark and cold, too bare, or too cluttered.

Common semistructural problems include uneven or rocky floorboards and poor wall surfaces, such as bad plasterwork or cracked or crazed tiles, and ceilings with missing moldings or damaged cornices. Woodwork can also be in need of a drastic face-lift. Doors often need to be replaced or refurbished, ugly fireplaces or other features can be oddly shaped, and badly placed windows can be eyesores. Even a wall in the wrong place can ruin your ideas for the room.

However, none of these faults are too difficult to cope with. Most design problems can be solved with the proper choice of color and a deft use of design technique and texture. Of course, any semistructural problems must be fixed adequately by you or a professional before you undertake any remodeling, refurnishing, or redecorating. Beautiful new wall coverings, fabrics, and paint will just peel off the wall if you have not let new plaster dry long enough, for example. Modern materials and techniques make it possible to do a great deal to rescue run-down surfaces from the ravages of time or the treatment of former tenants.

However, you may find you have more of a major disaster on your hands, especially if you have bought a run-down old property with possibly damp, dry, or wet rot; a leaking roof; plumbing that needs replacing; unsafe electric wiring; or falling-down plaster on the walls and ceiling. If this is the case, call in professionals to get the necessary help and advice you'll need before you attempt to do anything.

A qualified architect (or interior designer) or a good builder should be able to give you an idea of how these faults can be fixed and how much they will cost. Other professionals, such as roofing specialists and damp and decay experts, will also give free advice and estimates for work to be done, so do not hesitate to call them. If you plan to make any structural alterations of your own, it makes sense to check with a professional to discover exactly what you can and cannot do. You'll need to check the building codes in your area before you start work, for example.

Space—too much or too little—can also be a problem. You might have a wonderfully long hall or corridor but a tiny living room. You can, of course, change the shape of the rooms on any floor of a house by knocking down walls and making two rooms into one, or you can build walls elsewhere. This is something that requires the advice of an architect or general contractor since many internal walls are load-bearing and support either the floor or a wall in the rooms above. But remodeling the interior of your house in this way can help you make far better use of the available space. Other possibilities include building an extension, redesigning part of the rear of the property to create mezzanine levels linked by short staircases, or converting an attic room. All these ideas could transform your house; and professional advice is definitely needed at these critical planning stages.

RENOVATION

If ceilings, walls, floors, doors, woodwork, and windows are showing the ravages of time but are structurally sound, there are ways to renovate them. In some cases a cover-up job is the most practical and the most successful decoratively, but it depends on the actual problem and the type of surface you want to use as part of your basic scheme. There's no benefit to covering a cracked or heavily textured wall with wood paneling, for example, if you want to achieve an elegant traditional look—the paneling would be more suited to a colonial or country style. Instead, you could cover the poor surface with draped fabric in a moiré or watered silk and achieve the effect you want.

A cracked wall, ceiling, or wood surface is often accentuated by its painted surface or wall covering—shiny paints, metallic wall coverings, or pale, delicately textured paper will only emphasize the problem. A darker color, a heavier texture for the wall covering, a matte or textured paint, or a special painting technique will help to hide small faults and imperfections. A change of light source can also help. If you have poor walls, try focusing the main light up to the ceiling and using diffused pools of light from lamps. If the ceiling is in poor condition, combine soft background lighting with direct lighting to focus attention on interesting features. If you experiment with some portable fixtures, you can plan new lighting positions so that only diffused light falls on the problem area.

The best way to tackle ravaged surfaces is to begin at the top and work down.

Start with the Ceiling

Really bad plasterwork must be taken down because there is a very real danger of its falling down. If you are not too sure, seek expert advice and call in a plasterer to check it. The ceiling can be replastered or replaced with wallboard and painted or wallpapered to suit your color scheme. Avoid the temptation, however, of putting a rippled or heavily textured surface in place of the old. This is very difficult to remove. It may actually be one of your present problems. Covering up a poor ceiling with ceiling or acoustic tiles can also be a mistake; these can be very difficult to remove if you want a change of style.

If you have a ceiling that is not too bad structurally but has a decorative surface that is just not to your taste, you may be able to camouflage it quite successfully. A smooth but slightly cracked or bumpy ceiling can be covered with a special vinyl ceiling paper that has a linen-like texture and a fabric backing (not too difficult to remove if you want a change later) and then painted—a darker color and matte paint will help to disguise faults. If the ceiling is low, do not use too dark a color; this will just emphasize the lack of height. A boldly patterned paper is a good cover for uneven ceilings: Use one with a flowing, nondirectional pattern rather than one with a geometric design, which can be difficult to hang. A cleverly painted pattern can also help, particularly if there is only one bad area.

Wood covering, particularly in the form of tongue-and-grooved boards, blends equally well in both modern and traditional settings. For a very contemporary effect, try running the boards diagonally. Both methods will effectively cover a multitude of sins and can be removed if you decide on another treatment later on.

Tenting with fabric is another good way to cover up an ugly ceiling. It can look wonderfully romantic in a bedroom and sumptuously elegant in a dining room. You can even add a layer of insulation behind the fabric to help keep the room warm. Many of the companies who will hang fabric for you can provide a special insulating material for this purpose.

If you have an older house, there may be a dent in the ceiling where molding is missing or damage to part of the decorative plasterwork on the ceiling or cornice. Treatment depends on the extent of the damage—if it is very slight you may be able to repair it with a little trompe l'oeil by painting in the missing piece; or applying some filler may well be the answer. If the problem is more extensive, there are several ways of solving it. Many manufacturers make fibrous plaster copies of ceiling roses, moldings, and cornices, so you may be able to get a replacement that is virtually identical. It may mean replacing a run of molding if the seam is not to be too obvious. If your ceiling is more ornate and the pattern is one that is not popular enough to be copied, there are specialist plasterers who will make matching pieces to order—but look in the catalogues first.

Decorative ceilings are a marvelous architectural feature. If you have one, treat it with respect and restore it with care. If you color the "bed" (the flat part) and highlight the plasterwork in white or a light color to contrast, the effect will be even more dramatic.

You may not realize that you have beautifully decorated plasterwork above your head if the house is old and the details have gotten hidden behind layers of paint over the years. Cornices may just look rigid or bumpy and poorly textured. It is well worth the time and effort to remove the residue of paint, restoring any parts where necessary and then making sure any new paint does not fill up the indentations again. Many of today's water-based paints are suitable for ceilings, but do not use a shiny oil-based paint as it can be too reflective.

Timber beams, which are exposed in some older country houses, may also need restoring. If the problem is one of decay, call in the relevant expert. New pieces of timber can be spliced in with an invisible joint. In the past it was fashionable to use heavy stains or even creosote on wooden beams to preserve them. The stain can be removed and the beams then be bleached or sandblasted.

Continue with the Walls

Some of the problems with walls are the same as with ceilings. They often suffer from old bumpy or cracked plaster. But again, if the surface is in really bad condition, call on an expert for help and advice.

Quite a few of the cover-up techniques already suggested for ceilings will work well with walls, but if you want a plain painted surface or a beautiful, delicately textured wall covering, you must have a really good surface as a starting point. This may involve replastering some areas or covering them with wallboard or insulation board before decorating.

Remember that light colors and shiny and

delicate textures (paint or wall coverings) will highlight any imperfections. You may find you have to change your mind and use a different treatment from the one you first thought of and use a strongly patterned paper, for example, instead of having a plain surface. Or you can try altering the lighting (as suggested for ceilings); if direct sun and daylight shine strongly on the wall, filter it through light drapes or blinds or venetian blinds.

Most of the painting techniques, such as marbling, dragging, rag rolling, sponging and stippling, work extremely well and are a good disguise for a fairly bumpy wall surface.

Brick walls may be underneath plaster, and you can chip away the plaster to expose them. But make sure before you start work that the wall is brick and not just a partition wall of block, plasterboard, or timber. Once exposed, the brick should be cleaned and sealed. Walls can also be resurfaced using stone, brick, or slate, if this suits the type of house, style of decorating, and furnishing you intend.

If you already have wood paneling but it is too dark, stained an unpleasant color, or has been painted, try to strip it back to the bare wood and then varnish or wax it. Or, if natural wood just does not fit in with your design scheme, you can paint over it. However, if you have a very old house with genuine paneling, think very carefully before you do anything so drastic.

Occasionally what looks like fine old paneling is actually a 1920s or 1930s imitation called *scumbling,* where inferior wood is stained and glazed to simulate a particular wood grain and color, and you may only discover this after you have spent hours stripping the wood. If in doubt, call in the experts for an opinion before you start to work.

Crazed or discolored tiles can be another unsightly problem. You can retile on top of tiles, but not if they are cracked or broken (see pages 117 and 118). Any of the methods for covering up poor plaster can also be used for a tiled wall.

Get Down to the Floor

The floor may not really be a problem area—you may simply have difficulty in deciding what type of treatment to use on it and what floor covering to select. If the existing surface seems damaged, uneven, or damp, call in a professional flooring contractor to see what can be done.

A solid floor that is uneven, cracked, or pitted can usually be treated fairly easily with a leveling compound. The floor can then be treated as new and any suitable floor covering or permanent or semipermanent flooring placed over it.

Floorboards may be loose, creaking, or uneven because they have been lifted to lay wiring, heating ducts, or plumbing pipes. They can usually be screwed or nailed down to the joists beneath to secure them. Check on the location of pipes and wires before you start work. Gaps between boards that have shrunk can be filled with thin strips of wood; small gaps can be filled with wood filler or caulk.

Uneven floorboards must be made level. If they are not, the edges of the boards could work through any floor covering, causing it to split, crack, or fray. The best way to fix this problem is to make sure the boards are firmly attached to the subflooring, and then cover the entire expanse with a layer of plywood (rough side uppermost if you want a good grip for a new floor covering) or composition board, screwed into position. If you plan to lay a ceramic tile or other heavy floor upstairs, check on the strength of the joists to see whether they can take the added weight. Also make sure there is no movement in the floor that might cause tiles to crack or break. If you are at all unsure, seek the advice of an expert.

If the floorboards are sound but are painted or badly stained, one creative solution is to have them taken up and then relaid upside down. There may be some marking where the boards crossed the joists, but this should not be too difficult to remove by sanding. Otherwise, the boards can be stripped and sanded and are then ready for the decorative treatment of your choice. This can include painting, staining and sealing, stenciling, or even marbling.

If your floor is carpeted and the carpet is of good quality and in good condition, avoid the temptation of laying new carpet on top of old. Even laying new carpet on top of old underlay is a mistake, since the wear pattern transfers itself quickly to the new carpet.

Openings, Staircases, and Woodwork

The flesh on the bones of a room—the doors and windows, door handles and locks, stairs and handrail, fireplaces, and other built-in fixtures—all need to be architecturally right for your choice of interior design and the style of the residence.

Doors The wrong door can completely spoil a country-style room where the traditional doors were generally made of planked timber with a heavy latch and hinges. In some older houses, the original doors may simply have been covered up to provide an easy-to-decorate surface; so take the doors off their hinges and investigate.

When doors are used as dividers—between two parts of a large room or between two rooms that connect—it is even more important that they are seen as an integral part of the decorating scheme. If they are unattractive, think about changing them for doors that will fit into your plan, or decorate them so they merge into the background. Decorated doors can also brighten up dull areas such as long corridors. They can even be included in a fantasy painting in a child's or teenager's room, or as part of a trompe l'oeil in another setting.

Attractive doors in good condition can be stripped back to the natural wood and sealed. Plain doors can be decorated to look paneled, or molding can be added to simulate paneling. Many of the paint techniques are particularly suitable for doors. They can be decorated boldly so that they stand out from the background and become a focal point or treated in such a way that they blend into it.

Windows Windows and their treatments are discussed in detail on pages 89–101, but no number of sophisticated decorating techniques can disguise a window that is simply not right for a room. It is very much a question of style—the type of window should suit the architecture of the room and the way in which it has been furnished and decorated. In many houses the original windows have been taken out and new ones fitted that are totally unsuitable for the existing style. If possible, restore any existing windows or replace them with the appropriate style. You may need the advice of an architect to help solve the problem. Think about windows in relation to the façade of the house as well as the effect from inside the room.

Different-shaped windows all featured on one wall or a window that is cramped up in one corner can be replaced; the window openings can be made larger or smaller or the positions of them altered. There are other ways, however, of making visual improvements from the inside of the house that do not involve any major structural change (see pages 89–101). Care should be taken when changing windows to ensure that the effect is also good from outside and does not clash with the original architecture. A sliding glass door can do a lot to improve a dark downstairs room, creating a wall of glass that is less a window than a see-through wall and blends in nicely with many different types of homes. Windows or doors that lead out to a garden or onto a terrace in an older house, however, should be in keeping with the existing interior and exterior architectural styles.

Staircases These must be sound. If you have problems with creaks and groans, wobbly treads, or shaky banisters, get a carpenter or builder to check them out and carry out the necessary replacement or repairs. Damaged balusters can be removed and replaced. Copies of many different styles are readily available from lumberyards. Shaky handrails and banisters can be removed and a new unit of wood or wrought iron installed.

If the hall and landing are cramped or dark, replacing the stairs may well be the best way to solve the problem. Adapt your existing staircase or put in an open-tread staircase to let in a lot of extra light. A spiral staircase saves a lot of space as well as looking decorative. When a complete renovation is being considered, a staircase can be moved to allow for more space. It could also become an integral part of the living area, leaving the old hall and landing area for other purposes. Alternatively, the stair, hall, or landing area of a small house may become part of an open-

plan living room. In that case, it is important to choose treads, risers, banisters or balusters, and handrails very carefully, since they actually become part of the room design. The area can become the main focal point or be seen as a large piece of statuary and be highlighted with uplights. Altering the position of a staircase or installing a new one is a major undertaking. You will need to call in a qualified architect or a good carpenter to help you with your plan.

Camouflage

Tall Rooms

If you have a room that just seems too tall, try emphasizing the horizontal lines to take the eye away from the vertical ones. Highlight a picture rail and frieze above it in a color contrasting with the rest of the wall area and ceiling or cornice, for example. Or highlight a chair rail in the same color as the baseboards and any other horizontal trims. Contrast the two walled areas above and below the rail, using paint on one half and paper on the other. Alternatively, you can paint the areas in complementary colors, or use two coordinated wall coverings.

Try a patterned wall covering with a horizontal design, or perhaps hang a striped wallpaper horizontally across the room instead of vertically—the stripes need not be contrasting in color but can be quite subtle. Wall-to-wall curtains with a definite border or horizontal design can be effective. Try strongly colored floor coverings and furniture to lower the eye level.

Too-tall rooms can also be ideal for a split-level furniture design, which in turn helps to reduce the apparent height. In a multi-purpose room, a bed can be built on a raised platform with storage or a desk below. Similarly, a dining room could be separated from the living area by a change of level. Hanging ceiling lights quite low at regular intervals or clustering them at different heights can also be effective with very high ceilings.

Light the room inventively to draw attention to pools of light that focus on well-planned features in the room, such as a special collection of sculpture or glass. Always keep the ceiling in shadow or light, with diffused lighting hidden behind a horizontal valance.

Try any of these remedies before you do anything as drastic as putting in any form of false ceiling. Lowering the ceiling is not very effective and can spoil the proportions of a room.

Long, Narrow Rooms

If you feel oppressed in a long, narrow room, first try rearranging the furniture. If you do not want to have to move heavy sofas or chairs around the room you can figure out what will fit where by making a plan to scale (see pages 10–11). Try placing large pieces of furniture, such as a sofa, table, or row of cabinets, at right angles to a long wall so that they form a natural division. This will make the room seem shorter while allowing you to create an open space when it is needed for entertaining. Kitchens that are too long can be divided with fitted cabinets and work surfaces.

You can zone areas of a multipurpose room in this way. In a bedroom you can create a dressing area by dividing off part of the room with wardrobes and chests of drawers placed to face inward toward the dressing area. Back these with fabric or some type of wall covering or other decorative surface; they might

then form the headboard wall or some other feature. Any gaps on the side of the wardrobes or above the chest could be closed with vertical, venetian, or festooned blinds in colors to suit the scheme of the room. This treatment can also work well in a room that is shared.

Another way to create different areas is with varying floor treatments. You can treat the floor of the dining area or dressing area differently from that of the sitting or sleeping area, for example. Make it practical and washable in one area, perhaps using vinyl tiles, and softer and more relaxing underfoot in the other, by laying a deep pile carpet. If the floor is carpeted throughout, you can put a boldly designed or contrasting rug on top and group furniture around it to form a conversation area.

You can bring the ends of the room closer together by decorating them in a darker or stronger color, or using a boldly patterned paper or hanging wall-to-wall curtains on them. You can create a striped effect across a wall and window with a border in paint or paper on the wall, and a fabric border on the curtains. Another way to improve the room is to emphasize one of the long walls. In a bedroom it could be used for a row of cabinets, perhaps with mirror-fronted doors magnifying the apparent size and width of the room. If the wall is without recesses or projections, try making some niches or using wall-mounted shelves and unit furniture.

If you feel the room would look better with some kind of divider, use pale-colored screens, vertical blinds, or drapes, or glazed or solid folding doors.

Make an interesting feature of the floor by having stripes go across the width of the room. This can be done by painting or stain-

This long, narrow kitchen occupies space that is little more than a corridor. A strong color scheme helps adjust the balance, and a glossy painted floor rug defines the kitchen.

Intercepting the room's dominant vertical lines are the curved angles of the dining bank. Arranging furniture at an angle will soften a long, narrow room. The basically gray—with bright accents— color scheme includes the countertops and dining booth and table, and then continues up the stairs.

ing floorboards, laying carpet with a bold directional pattern across the room, or using two-tone tiles to create wide stripes. Border or inlay techniques can be used to outline specific areas.

Low Rooms

If your room is too low-ceilinged or the ceiling slopes and creates unusual angles, keep the room simple: Furnish it with floor cushions, divan beds, or low-slung seating.

Create a conversation or sleeping area. Buy small, neat pieces of furniture for a period setting.

Paint the ceiling a pale, cool color and the walls just a shade or two darker. Try giving the ceiling the vista treatment—decorate it to look like the sky seen through openings in billowing clouds, or pale stars on a very soft blue ground. When a ceiling slopes, it can be decorated with a mini-print pattern that diffuses the angles. Carry the pattern to the

Sometimes the best thing to do with an unusually shaped room is to emphasize what makes it distinctive. This small space was suitable only for something simple, either a single piece of furniture or some very small chairs and a table. Painting the walls a dark receding color and keeping the ceiling light has made this play space seem more like a room than a corner.

walls and coordinate it with the window treatment. So long as the colors are pale and the pattern self-effacing, the overall effect will not be overpowering. Coping with a slope can call for creative design solutions—such as trimming the edges of an angular slope with a border paper or a stenciled design.

Throw as much light as possible onto the ceiling—use uplights and paint the ceiling with a shiny or satin surface or, for a striking effect, use a reflective paper.

Tiny Rooms

Some contemporary houses, country cottages, and apartments have one or two very small rooms. Solve this design fault according to the function of the room. In some cases, emphasizing the small, cozy atmosphere may even be the answer. You can make a small dining room look more intimate by using rich, dark warm colors and soft textures but keeping patterns muted. Give a small bedroom an exotic look with a tented ceiling and fabric-draped walls in rich, warm colors. Make a study inviting with thick-pile carpets, subdued lighting (except for the desk lamp), and an expensive textured wall treatment such as suede or a suedelike fabric.

If your tiny room is the bathroom, you may be able to indulge your sense of the ridiculous, and decorate it with some interesting trompe l'oeil, such as a really interesting mural. You could put in small bookshelves or you could just use it as a collector's corner, tiling it with a patchwork of different tiles.

Keep furniture for small rooms neat and compact and use a mirror to face cupboard and wardrobe doors to double the apparent size of the room. A few well-chosen pieces of large furniture can make a small room appear larger. Breaking the room up with too many

Many apartment kitchens can be closet-size, making it difficult for even one person to use them. Eliminating any of the basic appliances is out of the question, so the only logical things to remove are doors and drawers. In this compact kitchen, a rack is fitted on to one of the walls to make up for lost storage space and provide easy access to often-used kitchen tools.

small pieces can have the opposite effect. Make any built-in furniture merge with the background by painting it all the same color or to match the background of the wall covering. Some of the more subdued painted-surface techniques particularly come into their own here, so long as they are done in pastel colors—try rag rolling or sponge stippling.

For small bathrooms, the cozy look can be translated into warm wood paneling on ceilings and walls. Try to expand the size of the room with light, shiny walls and ceiling treatments. Remember: Shiny surfaces reflect light and make an area look larger, but they do also show up any surface imperfections. In a bathroom, ceramic tiles or mirrors can be used very effectively to make the room seem larger. Light-colored glossy paint and foil wallpaper also look good. Cleverly designed shelving fitted around a cramped washbasin can be extremely useful for extra storage. You can increase the apparent size of the floor by taking tile flooring up onto the side of the bathtub. There are other flooring tricks that can be used in small rooms, such as painting the baseboards to match the floor or laying light- and dark-colored tiles alternately, to form a checkerboard pattern. Or "stretch" the room by laying tiles diamond-fashion, from corner to corner.

A striped floor laid diagonally will visually increase the size of a room. Use floorboards or a carpet with a diagonal design.

Basically, with small rooms, you should always keep the size of any pattern scaled down to suit the surface on which it is used, and choose pale, cool colors. Monochromatic color schemes also help make a small room look larger.

L-Shaped Rooms

Some rooms are long and narrow with a square fitted at the end—the traditional L-shaped room. These rooms are often spacious and elegant but can be difficult to furnish satisfactorily. Avoid the temptation to clutter them up with dividers, unless you need to cut off a corner for a particular reason, such as for a quiet study or hobby area.

You can use some of the furniture-arranging suggestions for long, narrow rooms in an L-shaped room. The color scheme should be planned as for one room to unify the two sections, although you can employ some of the foreshortening tricks to make it appear less long.

In some L-shaped rooms, the end of the "L" is too dark, and it is not always possible to install a window to let in natural light. Reflected light can be used here, either with mirrors or by putting glass panels in doors. Sometimes the narrow end of the "L" is an ideal place to build or position a wall of shelves and cabinets, which could then be lit by concealed lighting from above and bounced off mirrors on the wall at the back. It could also be the ideal position to feature a favorite large picture, wall hanging, or piece of designer furniture and have it highlighted with a spotlight.

Subtle, diffused lighting thrown up onto the ceiling by uplights can help with the balance of this type of room. The rest of the lighting for the room can come from strategically placed lamps and spotlights.

Try dividing the areas by contrasting floorings, as with long rooms, or by laying patterned flooring across the width if you need to play the widening trick. You can break up the floor area visually by laying flooring widthwise across the long part of the room and changing direction at the apex of the "L."

If an L-shaped room is fairly high-ceilinged, a raised platform with a railed gallery can make an interesting visual break and create plenty of storage space under the platform. This area can then be used for dining, sitting, or as a media center. If there is sufficient light, a really effective and dramatic treatment is to make the end of the room into a small garden, divided from the rest of the room with a tracery of arches or trellis, and filled with shrubs, trees, and plants lit by spotlights and uplights.

If an L-shaped room is a bedroom, the extra section could be the ideal place for a dressing room or bathroom. Attractive screens can be used to subdivide the area; alternatively, fitted cupboards can be built across it.

Strangely Shaped Windows

One semistructural problem is awkwardly placed windows or several different-sized or -shaped windows in one wall. It may not be worthwhile to alter the structure of the windows, and changes may not work externally. Window problems—different sizes, shapes, and treatments—are covered on pages 89–101.

Try not to cover up a window that has an interesting shape. All too often one of the irregularly shaped windows is beautifully proportioned and looks right in the room, while the others are ugly and perhaps too high or too low. The secret is to try to create a sense of unity. This can be done by covering the entire window wall with venetian blinds or floor-to-ceiling lace curtains combined with heavy overdrapes. Another possible treatment is to have well-chosen but false curtains to each side of the window wall, with a valance above. Companion or contrasting venetian, festoon, or roman blinds can be fitted to each window if appropriate. The most attractive window could be highlighted by painting the frame to contrast with the surrounding wall area, with the frames of the others painted to blend with the wall decoration. Blinds to match the wall treatment could be kept permanently closed if there is enough daylight in the room.

Some windows are so high up that they serve no purpose other than letting in a little extra light, or they may be circular and impossible to curtain. A collection of colored glass can be displayed in the window that will throw attractive, colored shadows onto floor or walls when the sun shines. A stained-glass panel, decoratively interesting in itself, is another possible solution.

Boxy Rooms

Many rooms are neither too high, too low, too long, nor too narrow—they are simply lacking in character. You can have a lot of fun adding atmosphere and style to rooms like this. Once again, the function of the room will influence your choice to some extent—and so will the basic style you want to create, taking into account the overall style of the house or apartment.

First of all, try to create a focal point in the room. This could be a fireplace or a large piece of furniture in a living room, the headboard or an interesting piece of furniture in the bedroom, or a window treatment in almost any room. In the right situation, a mural or decorative wall treatment can open up a square room completely. If you prefer a changing scene, group pictures or prints together, and move them around from time to time to give a different emphasis.

Interesting ceiling treatments will help alter the proportion of a room that is too square. You can use wood, tiles, or fabric, or paper or paint with an interesting pattern or design. Tented fabric ceilings look exotic in the right setting, such as in a bedroom or cozy study.

Making a feature of one wall is another good way of improving a characterless room. Wood, slate, brick or stone coverings will all work well where appropriate. Use a wall of furniture, feature books on display shelves in living areas, or put units with drawers or wardrobes with unusual door treatments in the bedroom. In the bathroom or kitchen try tiling one wall only—or do three walls plain and one with a special ceramic tiled panel. Emphasize windows on one wall by making dramatic floor-to-ceiling and wall-to-wall curtains, even if there is only one medium-size window, or try this effect with vertical blinds.

A creative floor treatment can also improve a boring room. Try using a definite bold pattern diagonally across the room from corner to corner, either by cutting and fitting floor tiles or painting, staining, or laying floorboards or solid floors. Carpet in a decorative way, or use vinyl flooring to form inlaid patterns. Outline features of a room—a group of furniture, bed, bath, or a row of cabinets—with a border design using tiles or sheet material in kitchens and bathrooms or carpet in living areas.

Triangle-Shaped Rooms

Some rooms are such strange shapes that they seem almost triangular. If you have a room that has a definitely tapered feeling or where one corner seems to dominate, try to disguise it by using pale colors and simple patterns on the two walls that form the "point" and treat the other wall more boldly in a strong color of paint or with a distinctly patterned wall covering. Alternatively, you can treat all three walls in a different way. Avoid fitting furniture into this type of room if possible, since this can emphasize the narrow end, but use wall-mounted corner cupboards, for example, to flatten out the corner. Arrange furniture in such a way that it creates the same effect. If you have a talent for painting or know an artist, you can paint a scene across the apex to flatten it out. Avoid patterns with straight lines and regular repeats in this style of room. The floor can have a fairly bold pattern on it, but consider a floral or in-

definite design for the other surfaces.

If you live in a large old house, the hall and stairwell may be cold and unwelcoming as well as being vertically triangular. Use a warm, bold color scheme, and try to emphasize the base of the triangle with an interesting treatment for the lower wall level and by selecting an unusual floor covering. Graduate the color of the wall above from dark to light, to minimize the apex effect. This can be done by painting the whole wall a midtone, and then stippling, rag rolling, or sponging with a darker and lighter color to make it lighter at the top and darker at the bottom.

Projections and Recesses

There are two ways of treating a room with many projections and recesses: either emphasize and make a design feature out of them or decorate to distract attention from them.

To emphasize recesses, make them into proper alcoves, where appropriate, with arched tops, built-in shelves, and concealed lighting, or make full use of them for decorative pieces of furniture. Treat the backs and sides of these alcoves differently from the surrounding wall area. If you want to distract attention from recesses, fill them with furniture, and decorate the alcove, the furniture, and the surrounding wall area with the same color, texture, or paint finish.

If the recesses are caused by a mantelpiece projecting into the room, it may be possible to flatten the wall. This is a structural job, however, and you will need to seek professional advice. If this is not feasible, then make a focal point of the fireplace, and carry the treatment around into the recesses. For example, echo the line of the top of the surround with a shelf or built-in cupboards in the recesses. Or stone-clad or brick-clad the fireplace to a suitable height, finish with a shelf, and take the shelf or cladding around into the recesses.

Take the emphasis away from the problem wall by highlighting the other walls. If a projection is part of a wall forming an arch between two rooms, you can emphasize it by painting or papering it a different color from the walls at right-angles, or by outlining the arch with a border or stencil pattern.

A SENSE OF STYLE

THERE ARE MANY DIFFERENT TYPES OF DECORATION that will give a room a specific style or atmosphere, from a traditional look to a country style to modern minimalist features.

Style can be created with a combination of the type of pattern used on the various surfaces of the room and the colors and textures selected. These are then imposed on the basic room, making allowances for its size, shape, and good and bad features (see pages 12–15). Start by detailing all of these. Look at the room and decide what to keep and enhance, and what to remove or disguise. You will then need to cope with the basic shell, selecting suitable patterns, textures, and colors for the floors, walls, ceiling, and woodwork and choosing suitable window treatment. Then consider major buys—furniture, storage units, appliances, and equipment. Finishing touches in the form of accents, lighting, and accessories will add the final gloss to the scheme. A selection of styles is delineated here to help you identify your likes and dislikes and determine whether or not your preferred style would suit your home.

Some rooms have a style built-in because of their interesting architectural features, while others have no personality at all once the contents are removed and the walls stripped for redecoration. The dullest room of all is the small box-shaped one with a door, one or two small windows, and no recesses or projections to provide interest. If you have a room with a strong architectural style, this may well dictate the type of decoration, furniture, and furnishings you use. With a room lacking in character, you have the freedom to transform the room completely and create whatever atmosphere you feel is right.

Traditional

If you want to achieve a traditional atmosphere in a room in a contemporary or older home, you will need to decorate it in a style relating to a specific historical period. Popular periods include Tudor, Georgian, and Regency. Original or reproduction furniture and accessories relating to these styles are available.

Colors

Classical, in keeping with the relevant period:

- Adam greens, Wedgwood blues, Etruscan terra-cotta with black
- Faded pastels, muted tones, and neutrals for Regency, Georgian, and other periods that were not overly ornate
- Rich Oriental colors, intense jewel colors
- Natural dyes for fabrics and furnishings

Furniture

Good antiques or reproduction furniture:

- Good wood pieces
- High-boys, semicircular tables, chaise longues, dining tables, and chairs
- Lavish or simply patterned upholstery according to the style of the period—brocade, velvet, silk, leather, embroidery
- Classic expressions such as painted furniture featuring lacquering, gilding, stenciling, or trompe l'oeil

- Built-ins, such as bookcases decorated with moldings, to suit the architectural style
- Beds of the period—Empire four-posters, for example
- Brass inlaid pieces

Patterns

- Will depend on the period and should be classical in origin
- Gothic, paisley, Oriental
- Formal stripes and florals
- Greek key, fleur-de-lis, Regency stripes

Textures

- Carved and gilded opulence for Baroque
- Smooth and matte with fine moldings for classical and Georgian
- Exotic woods and patterns as backgrounds to Chinese or African antiques
- Simple natural textures to re-create Quaker and Shaker atmospheres

Walls

- Patterned wall coverings, Classical stripes, or formal florals for Regency through to Baroque
- Tapestry or draped fabric for an exotic look
- Plain paint in eggshell or matte finish to set off classical cornices and fireplaces

The white paneling in this traditional living room contrasts with the black furniture and dark wooden stair railing. A variety of floral patterns decorate the rug, chair, and overstuffed couch. In the dining room, a painted trellis covers a portion of the wall.

- Paneling and border trims
- Painting techniques—marbling, dragging, sponging, and stippling—can enhance Classical or Rococo interiors

Ceilings

- Decorative with ornate moldings, cornices, coving, plasterwork
- Painted scenes or cloudscapes for the more ornate traditional styles such as Baroque, High Renaissance, or Rococo

Floors

- A polished wood, inlaid woodblock, or parquet floor is the essential element of authentic Classical elegance.

- Marble floors and stairs are right for most restrained, Classical interiors.
- Slate, flagstones, brick, or tile are best suited to Tudor and Shaker styles.
- Tiles laid in checkerboard patterns embody Georgian and Edwardian interiors.

Accessories

- Gilt on opulent mirror and picture frames, highlighting simple Regency furniture, ornaments, and antiquarian books
- Brass door handles, vases, beaten plates, or even a Buddhist temple prayer gong, according to traditional style chosen
- Dark wood and Hogarth frames

Rich colors radiate through this traditional dining room, the most vibrant of which is the red of the walls. The same jewel colors are found in the Oriental rug that covers the glossy floors.

- Mirrors have to be chosen carefully— with wildly ornate gilded scrolls and fruit for a Baroque interior or simpler for Regency or Georgian interiors.
- China and glass, such as beautiful vases
- Old Oriental pieces
- Dramatic flower arrangements
- Period lamps or chandeliers—plain for a Quaker room or with thousands of pendulous crystals for an ornate room
- Flowering trees in tubs for an Orangerie effect
- Oil paintings and early engravings and prints for a feeling of period

Colonial

The Colonial style is America's own "traditional." It is a unique mix of period styles such as Queen Anne, Chippendale, and Sheraton, and everyday elements of the eighteenth-century American home, such as spinning wheels and stone-walled fireplaces. The result is a style that is like so much else that is American—an amalgam of elements borrowed from other countries and cultures, accented by pieces or elements that are purely a product of this country. The style belongs to the 1880s, but it has remained enormously popular for homes even today, perhaps because Americans can claim it as theirs alone. It is rich yet filled with rough, basic materials, opulent and often heavy, yet elemental.

Colors
- Delicate tones
- Orange, pale pink, purplish red, blue, ivory white

Furniture
- A mix of styles and elements—claw-and-ball feet on plain American cabinets, for example, and Hepplewhite lines on late-nineteenth-century tables and chairs

Both of these rooms use Colonial design elements. Checks were a favorite Colonial pattern and the checked pattern of this dining room's painted wooden floor, as well as the curtain's checks, echo those found in the yellow, brown, and white quilt.

- Spinning wheels
- Chippendale, Federal, Sheraton, and Queen Anne elements on chairs, tables, china cabinets, and dressers
- Four-poster beds

Patterns
- Florals
- Botanical prints
- Designs from Queen Anne and Chippendale styles

Textures
- Ornate wood carving

- Rough materials such as stone
- Soft, thick fabrics and carpets

Walls
- Two-part "dado" treatments where a chair rail divides the wall vertically and the two halves are treated differently—in two colors, for example, or in wallpaper and paint
- Walls painted in solid colors and woodwork in light or white colors

Ceilings
- Plain paint—white or light-colored

The wing chair and sofa found in this living room may now be considered Colonial, but the original colonists brought many pieces of traditional European furniture with them, which local craftsmen then reproduced. Paintings, usually portraits of family members, were the wall decoration most often seen in Colonial homes.

- Chandeliers in a range of styles, usually made from marbled glass in a patinaed bronze frame

Floors
- Oriental carpets
- Patterned wall-to-wall carpeting

Accessories
- Oriental elements—Japanese bottles, platters, vases, China collections
- "Domestic" items—pincushions, baskets
- Heavily gilded mirrors

Country

This elegant, simple, and uncluttered style is traditional in feel and romantic in atmosphere. The look is achieved by the casual but orderly placing of good-quality furniture and neat floral prints that, although smart, have a homey, relaxed feel to them. A link with nat-

Furnishing a home in country style may be done inexpensively, with secondhand furniture purchased at tag sales. The fact that this bedroom's furnishings don't match exactly only adds to its charm. The sunny color scheme brightens a dark room and mixes yellow pastels the way a quilt might.

ural elements through the use of cotton and wood for upholstery, wooden furniture, and flowers and plants provide the country house with its style.

Colors

- Fresh and clear minty greens and blues, sunshine yellows
- Soft pastels, muted as in watercolor painting, such as pale gray, pale blue, apricot, or rich, natural-dye shades of rust, terracotta, mushroom, creamy white
- Faded Oriental

Furniture

- Lovingly polished good wood pieces—

chests of drawers, dressing tables, chairs, and tables

- Traditional pieces such as corner cupboards, refectory tables, and hutches
- Provincial stripes and patterned loose covers
- Windsor chairs, wooden rocking chairs
- Four-poster beds
- Blanket chests, library steps
- Gate-legged tables
- Elegant stripped pine, not too rustic
- Well-shaped, traditional mirrors

Patterns

- Full-blown floral designs or cabbage rose patterns drawn in botanical detail

Collections are a feature of country style. In this Connecticut country kitchen, a collection of wicker baskets hangs from ceiling beams, waiting to be used for storage, to serve food in, or to be filled with dried flowers.

- Faded traditional
- Delft-style tile designs
- Gothic
- Traditional ethnic
- Restrained stripes
- Good quilts

Textures
- Rich and soft but not too opulent
- Linens and restrained use of cotton or antique lace
- Raw silks for upholstery and cushions
- Cottons, natural fibers
- Smooth woolen fabrics
- Leather for books and upholstery
- Polished wood, polished metal

Walls
- Wood paneling or molding
- Patterned paper or fabric
- Matte or semimatte paint
- Richly textured wall coverings

Ceilings
- Some restrained decorative plasterwork
- Wood beams

Floors
- Polished wood or parquet
- Stenciled hardwood
- Flagstone, brick, or tile
- Rag or woven rugs in floral designs
- Tiles laid in checkerboard patterns

Accessories

- Silver, pewter, brass
- Good-quality crystal
- Dried flowers and grasses
- Earthenware
- Embroidered cushions
- Displays of good-quality china
- Prints, watercolors, oil paintings of landscapes, animals, portraits; brass candle-sticks, traditional lamps
- Log baskets
- Leather-bound books
- Lace and quilted bedspreads
- Discreet chandeliers
- Vases, collections of shells, miniatures, or semiprecious stones
- Flowers and plants

Victorian

This is a rather heavy and sometimes florid style that features a lot of gilt and brass, flocking and chenille, and intricate styling for furniture and upholstery. The style gives you a chance to be a little flamboyant or excessive with pattern. Treat ceilings dramatically and choose textures for their voluptuous feel.

Colors

- Rich, smoldering, deep dark colors

If this graceful velvet couch were set in the Victorian room in which it may once have belonged, the walls probably would have been decorated in elaborately patterned wallpaper and the windows covered in thick velvet drapes. In contrast to this comparatively spare modern setting, it seems all the more sensuous.

Floral patterns, much loved during the Victorian years, are scattered throughout this room, embroidered on cushions, painted on furniture, and framed in prints and pictures. Decorated in rich reds and strong greens, this living room has the opulent yet casual feeling of a Victorian country cottage.

- Rich reds, golds, madonna blues, strong greens
- Colors of natural dyes

Furniture
- Heavy with ornate fretwork and other carved decoration
- Dominating pieces for large rooms
- Richly polished ebony, mahogany, walnut
- Cane and bamboo
- Wrought iron combined with wood or glass

- Wicker or cast-iron furniture, overstuffed upholstery with fringes, tassels, and piping
- Leather chesterfields
- Ornate brass or gilt trimmings
- Suites of furniture
- Brass or cast-iron headboards

Patterns
- Flowing yet formal florals
- Bold, overblown florals
- Victorian Gothic geometrics
- Wide, formal stripes

Bathrooms became popular during Victoria's reign, so what better room to grace with velvet, lace, and ornate wallpaper? Note the stained-glass window, the gilded mirror over the sink, and the gilded bird cage with a plant in it. The window seat even has a lace petticoat.

- Botanically accurate drawings of plants such as acanthus

Textures

- Opulent and very tactile: velvet, chenille, flocking, lace, leather, intricately carved wood, and cut crystal
- Brass, gilt, iron, black lead
- Mirror and etched glass
- Leather, rattan, and cane
- Majolica ceramics

Walls

- Patterned wall coverings of the period
- Fabric covered, painted
- Chair rails and panels
- Heavy mantels above fireplaces
- Border and frieze trims
- Painting techniques such as marbling

Ceilings

- Decorative plasterwork, moldings, cornices

- Wood paneling and beams

Floors

- Tile, slate, and flagstone kitchen floors
- Polished or inlaid wood, parquet, Oriental, painted-on designs to look like carpet, tapestry, and rag rugs
- Plain and patterned carpet
- Marble
- Checkerboard and border effects

Accessories

- Stained and etched glass
- China and knickknacks
- Green plants
- Gilt and brass pictures, heavily framed prints, samplers, and lacework
- Fruit and flowers
- Lamps made from converted gas or oil lamps
- Fenders and fire irons
- Embroidered fire screens and pictures
- Assorted cushions

Mission/Arts and Crafts

The Mission style emerged at the beginning of the twentieth century. This style is now experiencing a new popularity because of its forthright approach to basic design standards. The arts and crafts movement in England, which promoted craftsmanship as the leading principle of good design, is central to the Mission approach. The style emanates from beautifully crafted, straight-lined furniture made from quality woods. The colors are warm, the designs are full of parallel lines placed in interesting patterns, and the materials are those of traditional craftsmen—honest woods, high-quality metals, and wrought iron. Mission-style rooms, such as those that Frank Lloyd Wright designed, are simple in approach yet warm in tone, basic yet inviting.

Colors

- Rich, earthy, and saturated
- Moss greens; wood tones such as bark browns, russet, wheat, and gold

Furniture

- Stickley-style quality-made wood pieces, well designed and constructed, such as straight, square chairs with wood joints and pegs showing

The extensive use of wood on the walls, ceilings, decorative elements, and in the rectilinear furnishings of this Mission/ Arts and Crafts period home, illustrate the simplicity of fine craftsmanship prized by the movement. Etched-glass doors have a tree pattern also found in the hallway's table lamp.

- Circular tables
- Small, portable tables
- Upholstered sofas

Patterns
- Geometrics
- Low-key designs that are in keeping with the simple look
- William Morris florals

Textures
- Quality, simple woods such as oak, chestnut, and willow

- Metals such as hand-hammered brass, copper, and pewter for hardware, wrought iron and hammered copper for fixtures
- Rough fabrics such as burlap and coarse linen
- Leather for upholstering wood pieces

Walls
- Discreetly patterned wallpaper, often in William Morris designs
- Simple tapestries

When walls were not covered in wood, they were often decorated with one-of-a-kind flowered wallpaper, as is this corner.

- Paneling
- Restrained stenciling

Ceilings
- Plain, light paint
- Wood beams

Floors
- Rugs with geometric patterns
- Navajo throw rugs
- Dark plank floors

Accessories
- Functional items such as clocks and lanterns
- Baskets
- Wood-framed mirrors
- Wrought-iron candlesticks
- Pottery

Art Deco

The name for this style originated at *Exposition Internationale des Arts Decoratifs et Industriels Modernes* in Paris in 1925. Art Deco attempted to eliminate the excessive decoration popular in the Art Nouveau movement with simpler, uncluttered items often designed for mass production. It was inspired in part also by the bright and more geometric designs of the costumes of the Ballets Russes when they appeared in Paris in the early 1900s and fulfilled the need for a new direction in design and the use of color. Elements of Art Deco were used right through into the 1930s, typified by the glamour of oceangoing liners and the cinema.

Colors
- Fresh pastels—peach, light blue, neutral and natural colors
- White and off-white
- Black, white, and gray
- Some rich, dark colors
- Sharp accents
- Some primary colors
- Gold and silver

Furniture
- Streamlined or swirling geometric shapes
- "New" materials such as glass, early plastics such as Bakelite

- Fur, leather, or canvas used for upholstery
- Printed and woven fabric loose covers
- Unadorned wood
- Painted items
- Exotic woods, such as satinwood and bird's-eye maple for bedroom suites

Patterns

- Mostly structured geometrics but early Art Deco style includes sylphlike, stylized women and floral or foliage motifs
- Early abstracts

Textures

- Opulent satin, silk, velvet
- Glossy ceramic, glass, chrome, other metals
- Matte and shaggy furs or pile carpet
- Bleached woods
- Stained, ebonized items
- Leather, wool tweed, canvas

Walls

- Plain paint
- Decoratively painted with wall patterns in geometric style, some murals

A popular decorative style of the 1920s and 1930s, Art Deco was characterized by bold outlinings, streamlined and rectilinear forms, and the use of new materials such as plastics. All of these modern rooms have achieved an Art Deco look by using different elements of the style. As a reaction to the excessively ornate decades that preceded it, Art Deco favored sleek silhouettes such as those found on this dining room furniture, which is crafted in exotic woods with a highly glossed finish.

Favored Art Deco patterns were geometric, as this living room illustrates. The diamond patterns found on the chairs are also found on the walls and on the cabinet doors.

- Patterned paper
- Glass panels
- Marble
- Wood panels, natural or painted
- Fabric-covered
- Mirrors

Ceilings
- Plain paint
- Streamlined plasterwork
- Beams
- Illuminated

Floors
- Stripped board

- Tile, marble
- Plain and patterned carpet
- Rugs—especially large circular ones

Accessories
- Decorative light fittings in glass or metal, the classic Art Deco design featuring a woman holding a lighted sphere
- Glass and china figures, clocks
- Statuary
- Plants, distinctive flower arrangements
- Satin cushions
- Etched glass

Modern/Minimalist

The essence of this type of design is functionalism. It is a paring down of ornamentation until a streamlined, almost spartan interior is created, with everything in its allotted place. Simple, unadorned shapes have to be selected with care, and the quality of all surfaces must be superb, even if some are textured and appear to be basic and unpretentious. Take as your guide the classic esthetic simplicity of Japanese interiors.

Colors
- Cool pastels
- Neutrals
- Natural colors for natural items
- Some splashes of restrained primary color

Furniture
- Well-designed, functional items
- Modern or traditional

This minimalist dining room takes its esthetic cue from the Japanese. Sliding doors separate it from the kitchen, and the no-fuss design persuades you to focus on the materials used—a glossy monochromatic scheme of glass, wood, tile.

Bare-bones functional is the best way to describe this modern/minimalist room. There's a place to sit and something to sit on—four white chairs that don't detract from the architectural beauty of the space. Everything in this room is essential.

- Streamlined shapes
- Practical multipurpose
- Classical

Patterns
- Should be confined to two or three surfaces
- Classical or geometrical

Textures
- Should be contrasting to add interest
- Matte with shiny, rough with smooth, chrome, brushed aluminum, or mirrors with ceramic finishes
- Decorative woods

Walls
- Plain paint, painted textures
- Wall coverings in suitable patterns
- Fabric, wood, or laminate-clad
- Faced mirror or special decorative glass

Ceilings
- Plain paint, painted textures

- Decorated sparingly with moldings
- Wood-clad
- Illuminated

Floors
- Marble, tile
- Wood of all types
- Plain, patterned, or bordered carpet
- Dhurries, hand-tufted specials, and Oriental rugs
- Sheet vinyl, sometimes inlaid
- Border effects
- Smooth-textured and studded rubber
- Finely woven sisals or mattings

Accessories
- Foliage plants, shrubs in pots
- Impressive flower arrangements
- Classic collections
- Period antiques, carefully arranged
- Well-lit modern paintings, photographs, and prints

Eclectic

This look is for those who like a variety of styles and buy accordingly. It works when bits and pieces are put together imaginatively, mixing old with new, taking great care to get the look right in unexpected juxtapositions. The furniture and backgrounds can be simple, with all the interest created by means of the accessories, although unusual wall paintings and craft objects can be an integral part of the eclectic style. It is a style for the individual, with no hard-and-fast rules.

Colors
Brash and bright in original combinations; ethnic, neutral, clashing, contrasting, toning, graduated, or dark and rich to suit the room and your particular set of furniture

Furniture
Almost anything goes, and styles can be mixed together:
- Leather
- Wood

- Glass
- Chrome and other metals
- Canvas chairs
- Overstuffed upholstery
- Overdecorated items
- Streamlined pieces
- Kitsch items adapted and used as furniture—jukebox, treadle sewing machine table
- Triple mirrors as headboard
- Modern classics such as Le Corbusier and Mies van der Rohe chairs or tables
- "Found objects" used as sculpture—shock absorber from a truck, shell as an ashtray

Patterns

- Art Deco
- Art Nouveau
- 1920s and 1930s geometrics
- Ethnic
- 1940s and 1950s to contemporary
- Animal skins

While some people strive for an eclectic look, it simply happens to others. No matter how hard some people work at a definite style, their homes can't help but reflect their own tastes and interests. This comfortably eclectic Santa Fe living room has traditional furniture covered with Native American rugs. Collected art ranges from a modern abstract painting to primitive pottery.

Why settle for one wall color when you can have a palette's worth? The artist who visualized this apartment decorated the living room walls with a patchwork of colors that would have made Picasso feel right at home. The Caribbean color scheme fuses the apartment's eclectic collection of traditional, contemporary, and one-of-a-kind pieces.

Textures
- Rough, harsh, homespun
- Shiny, matte
- Opulent or metallic

Walls
- Patterned wall coverings
- Fabrics
- Plain painted
- Decoratively painted
- Covered with collections or posters
- Trompe l'oeil
- Bare or textured plaster

Ceilings
- Decorative and beamed
- Painted plain or with special techniques
- Clad with tile or trellis
- Illuminated
- "Tented" with fabric

Floors
- Wood
- Tile
- Plain or patterned carpet
- Painted plain or patterned (solid or wood)
- Geometric or fairly sparsely patterned modern rugs
- Rubber
- Linoleum
- Sheet vinyl

Accessories
- These are a mixture of all types, modern and traditional, and should be massed together in a collection
- Paintings
- Sculptures
- Vases
- Uplights, wall lights, spotlights

Contemporary/Postmodern

Once, when we used the word *modern*, we meant "today." Now what is considered "modern" is from the past—chrome, leather, glass, and other elements of a bare, functional style that has now taken its place as just that—a style among others from the past. Modernism has long ago been replaced with a contemporary style, including postmodernism, that rebels against the cold aloofness of modernism. Postmodernism in architecture and design has meant incorporating enduring classical elements from the past into the context of contemporary design. So neoclassical elements such as columns, arches, stone and marble elements, and friezes have been prevalent—interpreted for contemporary schemes. Ornamentalism is also back—in an appreciation for architectural detailing such as arching windows, decorative moldings, intricate gates, and carved wood fireplace mantels. Today craftsmanship is valued, and the materials of it are everywhere—wood, metal, wrought iron, glass, tile. Decorative detailing is big—with special paint techniques from the past and a general celebration of color and pattern. This does not mean that subtlety does not exist within the postmodern style, however. In fact, many of these elements borrowed from the past are put into contemporary settings in the most sparing and restrained ways, using just a hint of them to bring life, softness, or humanity to a space.

Colors
- Bright, saturated tones—high-voltage hues used carefully
- A whole range of neutrals to balance out the brights
- Earth tones in new, sophisticated hues
- "Environmental" greens and blues

Furniture
- "High-touch" items made from tactile and unusual materials such as laminates, concrete, rubber
- "Neoclassical" furnishings such as Empire recliners and scrollback chairs, Biedermeier bird's-eye maple tables and dressers, tables and desks with columns for legs

Patterns
- Ethnic cloths and fabrics
- Textured looks made from special paint techniques that simulate wood, stone, marble, or create interesting patterns with sponges, combs, or just "spattering" on paint
- Stenciling
- Classical designs, such as the Greek key, where neoclassical elements are used

Textures
- Soft, flowing fabrics and animal skins for neoclassical settings

The fireplace in this living room/music room and the doorway in this dining room are characteristic of the architectural details that postmodern architecture restored, after years of spartan modernism. The model of an ancient Grecian structure on the fireplace pays homage to the classical forms that postmodernists admire.

- Tactile materials—paint techniques that make walls interestingly textured; the cool, firm feel of tile

Walls

- Heavy use of trompe l'oeil, faux finishes, and other historic paint techniques
- Stenciling
- Pastels to fit in with neo-fifties looks
- Draped with fabric for neoclassic settings

Ceilings

- Trompe l'oeil clouds and rosy sunsets
- Fabric "tents" for neoclassic settings
- Restoration of crown moldings and other architectural features or installation of new ones with foam "moldings" that look real when painted over

Floors

- Stenciling running around the room or down a stair
- Tile in vibrant colors and designs
- Faux or trompe l'oeil effects—a "stone" floor or one that has broken pottery painted to look real
- Colorful rugs, some patterned to look like mosaics

Accessories

- "Found objects"—a mahogany bowling ball, shock absorber from a truck
- In neoclassic settings, clocks that look like miniature buildings, vases that look as if they have stories to tell
- Collections of anything—pieces of tile, glass, shells, bottles, pillows

Southwest

The Southwest style is informed by the burnished earth and deep blue sky tones of the landscape and the vibrant influences of Native American and Hispanic cultures of the American Southwest. Part of the style reminds one of cowboy movies about the Wild West, with references to horses, wagons, and pioneers, but part of it is pure nature, with a respect for elements of the outdoors that can find a home inside—feathers, animal skulls, pottery made from rich clay. Handcrafted items also have an important place in the style, from artwork like oil paintings and sculpture that express the spirit of the area to functional items such as beautiful and unique Navajo rugs and blankets, handmade baskets, and metal pieces.

Colors

- Rich earth tones
- Neutrals
- Bright, glowing oranges, blues, and reds

Furniture

- Leather-upholstered chairs and sofas
- Spanish-influenced wood pieces—carved and paneled armoires, rope-legged chairs, tables with leather tops
- Southwestern interpretations of Biedermeier-style furniture—pine armoires and chests with classical lines
- Folk-tradition benches, settees, and tables with tapered legs and simple lines
- Sculptural "crafts" pieces

Green-painted wicker chairs, a Navajo rug in sun-baked colors, a blanket inspired by the desert sunset—all supply the glowing colors found in a blooming desert oasis. The room's molding and woodwork are painted white so that they stand out against the sage walls, accentuating the room's Southwest character and architectural features.

Patterns

- Navajo designs
- Stylized sunbursts
- Squares and rectangles, "stepped" designs

Textures

- Rope and matte materials
- Leather
- Rough woods
- Fur for covering seating surfaces

- Cane for chairs
- Knobby, woven fabrics

Walls

Plain stucco or painted in neutral tones, richly decorated with American West paintings and Native American–style wall hangings

Ceilings

- Plain painted
- Wood-beamed

Floors

- Stained hardwood planks
- Large Navajo area rugs

Accessories

- Handcrafted items—pottery, baskets, woven rugs and blankets
- Original Native American sculpture
- Handcrafted metals—wall sconces, sculpture, candlesticks
- Wild West items—saddles, buffalo heads

This Southwest kitchen–family room uses materials that harmonize with local elements. Adobe walls, which traditionally were white, are painted a sandy golden color to harmonize with the floor tiles. Except for the glossy work surface, the wood used looks unvarnished, sunbleached.

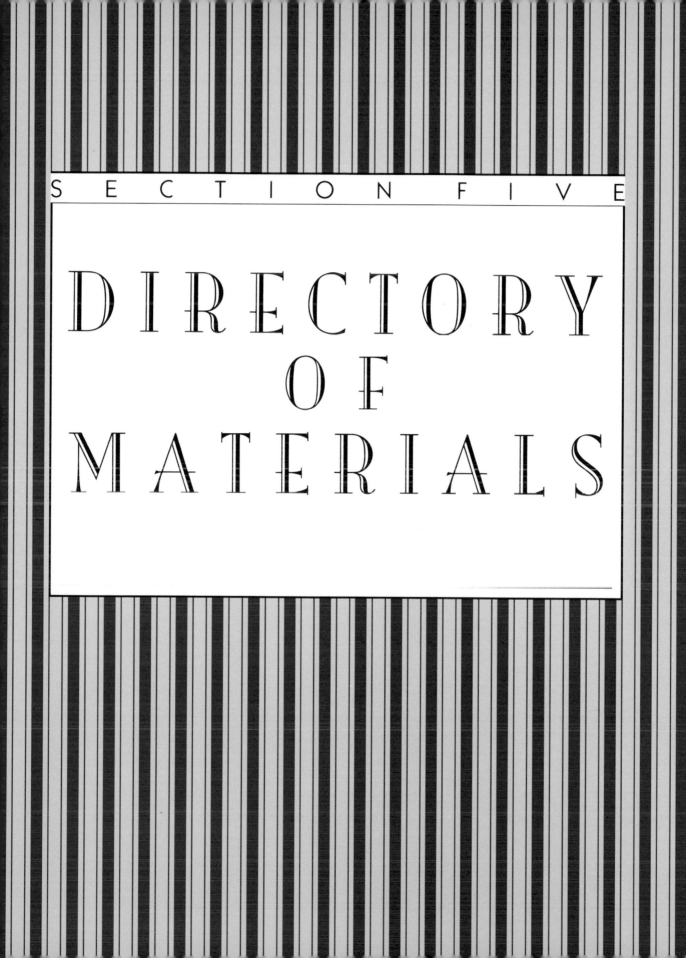

SECTION FIVE

DIRECTORY OF MATERIALS

A COMPREHENSIVE RANGE OF TYPES OF PAINT, fabrics, wall coverings, flooring, and lighting fixtures is presented in this section. Before buying any materials, make sure you calculate accurately the quantity required, allowing for a certain amount of waste. If you are buying an expensive item, such as quarry tiles for a large area, take advantage of any measuring facilities offered by the store. In the case of quarry tiles, it is difficult for the nonexpert to estimate how many additional tiles will be needed for going around corners and into cupboards. Whatever you are buying—wallpaper, paint, or fabric—it is essential to buy enough materials at the beginning to complete the job. Paint colors, fabric dyes, and tile colors will vary from batch to batch and you can never guarantee that you will find more of the same batch if you run out halfway through the job.

Floor Coverings

Hard Floors

Any hard flooring must be laid on the correct subfloor, which should be strong, level, clean, smooth, and moisture-proof. Many existing hard floors, such as floorboards, can be refurbished so long as they are in good condition (see pages 122–23).

Most of the floorings in this section are difficult to lay and best left to the professionals, although some of the wood floors can be laid successfully by a do-it-yourselfer.

Bricks and paving   Used mainly for patios, walkways, and garden rooms, they are also found in some older homes on the ground floor, laid directly on the earth. They come in natural, attractive brick colors from which patterns and borders can be created. The herringbone pattern of laying is most common.

Ceramic tiles   In different sizes, shapes, and thicknesses, ceramic tiles are used on floors in bathrooms, kitchens, utility rooms, and patios. They may be found in halls in older homes. Most types are glazed and are impervious to water and most liquids. Make sure you choose floor or multipurpose tiles— wall tiles are not strong enough. Select frost-proof tiles for patios, balconies, and sun rooms. These are very heavy; before installing them on upper floors, check how much weight the joists can take.

Flagstones   Found in some older homes on the ground floor. These may be laid directly on earth and can be restored and sealed.

Floorboards   You will find floorboards already laid on upper and lower levels in many types of houses. If they are in good condition, they can be sanded and sealed; stenciled; painted plain or patterned with floor paint; stained and sealed; or treated to one of the special painting techniques, such as marbling.

Marble   Used particularly in elegant European-style and old traditional houses, marble comes in several attractive natural colors and in many different shapes and sizes. It can be laid plain or in unusual or traditional patterns. Marble is heavy, so check that the joists can take the weight before laying on upper floors.

Mosaics   These can be made up of glass, marble, or ceramic pieces, usually slightly irregular in shape. Some come with a paper or mesh backing in 6-inch and 12-inch squares for ease of laying. Mosaic pictures or patterns should be planned in advance on graph paper and laid individually. Like marble, mosaics are heavy, so check that the joists can take the weight before installing on upper floors.

Slate   A quarried material, slate comes in gray-green and other natural colors. It is available in random shapes or as paving slabs. It is very heavy and must be embedded in a cement or concrete subfloor. It is too heavy for use on upper floors.

Stone   Stone is not used much nowadays, although it is found on the ground floor of some older homes. It comes in many different colors and thicknesses, and many regions have a local stone. It is usually square or rectangular. Some types need sealing before laying. Stone is a heavy material to use.

Terrazzo   Usually made from marble chippings and ground or polished, terrazzo is set in cement or polyester resin. Color, texture, and shape vary, although it is usually sold in square or rectangular slab form. It is a heavy material to use.

Wood floors   Hardwood strip, parquet, and floorboards are among the types of wood floors you will find. Different types of wood are used, and shapes and sizes vary according to the product. Prices also vary according to thickness, pattern, and timber used. Wood floors can be a very decorative and elegant flooring and, once sealed, are easy to care for.

Semihard Floors

Like hard floors, semihard floors are usually attached to the subfloor. Poor floorboards can be covered with plywood or flooring-grade chipboard, rough side down to give a level surface and to assist adhesion of the new flooring, which must be level, smooth, and moisture-proof. Some semihard floors are laid flat and require only stapling, usually in doorways or where they may be dislodged easily.

All of these types of flooring can be laid by a professional or an experienced do-it-yourselfer.

Linoleum   An old-fashioned flooring, linoleum can be repaired and polished or sealed if it is in good condition.

Rubber   Rubber is very bouncy underfoot and cuts down on noise. It comes in tile or sheet form in a range of subtle colors. Textured types are nonslip. It is generally used as commercial flooring.

Vinyl   Available in sheet and tile form, vinyl comes in various widths and several thicknesses. Cushioned vinyl has air bubbles trapped between the wear layer and the backing, which gives the flooring thickness and bounce. It is made in many designs and patterns—often simulating other traditional floorings such as wood, ceramic tile or slate, with varying degrees of success. Many of the tiles are self-adhesive and are easy to install.

Soft Floor Coverings

These are made from various fibers and include carpets, rugs, and matting. They are usually fitted directly onto the subfloor, or loose-laid on top of any of the floors described above.

Fitted wall-to-wall carpets should be professionally installed, especially on staircases. Rugs and loose-laid tiles can be put down by an experienced do-it-yourselfer.

Most types of carpet need a good underlay:

Never lay new carpet on old underfelt or old carpeting. Sometimes the underlay is built-in in the form of heavy foam backing; otherwise, you will have to buy it separately. Many types of underlay are available—felt, foam, rubber, and latex. Ask your dealer which one is best for your floor covering and existing floor.

Axminster carpet This carpet is made of cut-pile tufts placed in position as the backing is woven in. Fibers and blends of fiber vary and different pile effects can be produced. Many colors and patterns are available, and the carpeting comes in narrow widths and broadloom (made on a wide loom).

Bonded carpets A sheet of surface pile is bonded onto a backing and then cut to make a bonded carpet. The fibers are usually synthetic and can be blended with other materials. The colors are often plain and the widths are broadloom.

Matting Harsher underfoot than carpet, matting is usually made of natural fibers such as sisal, hemp, rush, or coir (fiber made from coconut husks). The colors are also generally natural, although some mattings are dyed. They may be seamed and fitted, broadloom and rifted, or bound and used as rugs.

Needlefelt/needlepunch carpets These can have a texture like cord or felt and are usually made with synthetic fiber. Different patterns and colors are available and the widths vary.

Rugs Rugs can be woven by hand or by machine, using the various methods described above for carpets. Rugs originate from many different countries, and those from the East or Orient can be particularly valuable. They include: Persian (Saraband, Kerman, Khilim); Caucasian (Soumak, Kuba, Cashmere); Turkoman (Turkestan, Afghanistan); Turkish; Dhurrie; and Chinese. European and American rugs include rag rugs, hand-pegged, hand-tufted, and tapestry. Colors and patterns are infinitely varied as are sizes, shapes, and textures. Rugs will usually be placed on top of one of the other floorings. An underlay is unnecessary, but make sure that rugs placed on a polished floor have a nonslip backing.

Tufted carpets To make a tufted carpet, tufts are placed into a woven backing and secured on the reverse side with a latex coating. The fibers and blends of fibers vary. These carpets are available in different widths and plain or patterned colors. Tufted area rugs, including some hand-tufted, are also available.

Wilton carpets The surface pile of Wilton carpets is woven in a continuous thread with the backing for strength and taken to the base when a new color is included. Fibers and blends of fiber vary, but Wiltons often contain some wool. The pile can be textured, plain (velvet), or carved. These come in plain or multicolors and are available as widths for seaming for wall-to-wall carpets and broadloom.

Paint

There are two basic types of paint—oil- or alkyd-based and water-based (latex). When you buy paint always read the small print on the can first to make sure it is the right paint for the job, check the coverage, and see whether any undercoat or preparation is needed. When undercoat is recommended, use the color recommended and made by the same manufacturer. If you have a large area to cover, make sure you buy paint with the same batch number because the color may vary slightly from batch to batch. If paint is being mixed to achieve a special shade, get all the paint you need mixed at one time.

Custom-tinted paint   Available in a wide range of colors, this tinting system involves mixing paints together. The paints are oil- or alkyd-based or water-based and come in gloss, luster, matte, and silk vinyl finishes. For each color shade, pigment is added to the relevant base. The can is then shaken mechanically to blend the pigment into the base and achieve the desired shade.

Gloss level   This refers to the amount of shine in the paint. There are five gloss levels: flat or matte (which has no gloss), eggshell, pearl, semigloss, and high-gloss or enamel. In general, high-gloss paints are appropriate for high-moisture and high-traffic areas, such as the bathroom. Flat finishes are harder to keep clean. Most people use low-gloss or flat paints on walls and semigloss or high-gloss paints on trim.

Latex/emulsion   A water-based paint, it has either a matte finish or a slight sheen. Available as free-flowing or gel (nondrip), it is used for interior walls and ceilings and is also available for external use. New developments include textured emulsions and solid emulsion that comes in a block and is particularly useful for painting ceilings.

Masonry paint   This tough emulsion is specially formulated for use on exterior walls. Most masonry paints contain mold and algae inhibitors, and some have additives to improve coverage and durability. Masonry paint creates a textured surface.

Multipurpose paint   This oil-based paint can be used on wood and metalwork as well as ceilings and walls inside the home. It has a gloss or semigloss finish and contains silicone and polyurethane, making it tough and flexible. An added advantage is that brushes used to apply this paint can be washed out under the tap.

Primer   A special type of paint, primer is formulated to protect new or exposed wood or metal surfaces. It is applied before the undercoat or topcoat. Stabilizing primers are also available for sealing damp, flaking walls.

Textured paint   A water-based paint, it gives a thick, gritty texture to walls and ceilings. It is usually applied with a roller or special spreader. Once applied it can be difficult to remove.

Undercoat   Oil-based undercoat is specially formulated for use with oil-based top-coat paint for woodwork and metal. Always use undercoat and top-coat paint from the same manufacturer to ensure the correct shade.

Wall Coverings

A wide range of wall coverings is available in paper, vinyl, and fabric and in many different colors, patterns, and textures. These coverings can be divided into two categories: flexible and rigid.

Always buy enough wall covering to complete the job, allowing for waste. Make sure that all rolls or lengths have the same batch number, because the color or shading may vary from batch to batch. Unwrap all rolls and check before starting to decorate.

Flexible wall coverings

Borders   Narrow bands of paper or vinyl wall covering, borders are used to outline features such as picture rails or to form decorative divisions. They can be coordinated with wall coverings or with plain painted walls.

Embossed wall coverings   These are also called relief wall coverings or "whites." They are made from white compressed paper/pulp to form a heavily textured surface that can cover many imperfections or uneven plastering. They come in many textures and are hung in the same way as wallpaper and then overpainted. Some heavy types are sold in panels. Embossed vinyls are also available.

Fabric   Fabric can be used to cover walls and ceilings. Some fabrics are specially treated and made extra-wide for this purpose. The types of fabric that can be used are numerous and include burlap, upholstery fabric, velvet, and even silk. They can be stuck, stapled, battened on, or fixed by special track to the wall. They are normally sold by the yard or, if paper-backed, by the roll.

Felt   Available in many colors, felt can be used to cover walls. It can be fixed as fabric. Special paper-backed felts are also produced and are hung like paper. Felt is sold as fabric by the yard or paper-backed by the roll.

Flocked wall coverings   These velvety-textured wall coverings come as paper, foil, or vinyl and some are prepasted. The designs and colors are suitable for traditional schemes.

Hand-blocked or hand-painted wallpapers   These are available with exclusive and expensive designs; special designs can be commissioned. Some of these papers are not colorfast so they will need professional handling.

Ingrain or wood-chip   A white wallpaper with wood or other chippings incorporated into the pulp to give it a textured finish, ingrain or wood-chip is hung vertically and overpainted. It is particularly useful for concealing defective wall surfaces.

Lining paper   This paper is used to give a smooth base layer either for other wall coverings or for paint. If another wall covering is to be hung over the top, the lining paper is hung horizontally—this is called cross-lining. If the wall is to be painted, it is hung vertically.

Metallics   Made from metallicized plastic film on a paper backing, metallics are hung like paper, using fungicidal paste. Light switches should not be placed over foils or metallics.

Natural textures   These textures include grass cloths and cork. They are usually paper-backed and hung as paper. They are sold by the roll or by the yard.

Standard printed wallpaper   This comes in a wide range of patterns, colors, and textures in standard rolls. Some types are washable and some are prepasted.

Suede and woven textile coverings   These are both produced with a paper backing and hung like wallpaper. They come in a wide range of colors and the woven textile coverings have a textured finish. They are normally sold in rolls and occasionally by the yard.

Vinyl wall coverings   Available in a wide range of styles and textures, they consist of a vinyl layer incorporating the plain color or pattern, which is then printed on a paper or fabric backing. The fabric-backed vinyls are particularly suitable for kitchens and bathrooms because they are highly water-repellent. A heavy texture to create the illusion of fabric can be incorporated. All are durable and washable, and some are prepasted and easy-strip. Heavy *contoured* or *blown* vinyl wall coverings are also produced, sometimes simulating ceramic tiles or natural textures. Vinyl is usually sold by the roll, but some fabric-backed ones are sold by the yard.

Rigid wall coverings
Ceramic tiles   Available in a very wide range of styles, sizes, patterns, colors, and even textures, ceramic tiles are usually glazed to make them impervious to water, steam, and condensation. Tiles are fixed to the wall with adhesive and the spaces between the tiles are grouted. Some tiles have several glazed edges, and are self-spacing to make fixing easier. They are usually sold by the

square foot. Mosaic wall tiles are available already spaced on a flexible mesh backing.

Cork   Available in tiles and panels, or bonded to paper, cork comes in both natural and dyed colors and has an attractive texture. It is ideal for kids' rooms because it serves as a bulletin board and provides good sound insulation. Cork is fixed in position with tile adhesive and should be sealed if the area is steamy or damp. It is sold either by the square yard or as single packs of tiles.

Mirror   Mirror is available as panels, individual tiles, and mosaics. Sizes vary considerably and some mirror glass is colored, textured, patterned, or etched. The tiles often come with adhesive pads. The surface to be covered must be smooth or flat to avoid distortion of image. Mirror is sold by the square foot or as individual panels.

Plastic laminates   Available in a variety of colors, patterns, and textures, plastic laminates may be made to simulate brick, stone, ceramic tiles, or wood. Alternatively, fabrics can be laminated to allow for coordinated schemes. Laminate is usually bonded on to a backing, such as chipboard, to form panels and is attached to the wall. It is very useful for covering up old tiles or a poor surface. Some preformed panels that lock together are also available for bathrooms and kitchens. Sold by the square yard or as panels.

Wood paneling   This comes in several forms. It is available as panels or tongue-and-groove planks that fit neatly together. Woods and colors vary, but usually wood has to be stained and sealed, oiled, or wax-polished after hanging. Wood is usually fixed by means of blind nails, but it can be stuck on with contact adhesive. It is usually sold by length or by the panel.

brick, slate, and stone. They either come as wall facings, or in their "raw" state. Most are difficult to put up and require professional installation.

Other rigid wall coverings   These include

Fabrics

Furnishing fabrics are made from various natural, synthetic, and combination fibers. Natural fibers are those made from vegetable and animal materials, such as wool, linen, silk, and cotton. Synthetic fabrics, such as acrylic and polyester, are produced by mixing chemicals with raw materials. Some fibers are more versatile than others, and at the moment there is no one particular fabric or fiber that can be used in every situation. When selecting a fabric, consider the job it has to do and the amount of wear it will get.

Key to Chart	
n/r	not recommended
✓	suitable
△	but can crease

FABRIC TYPE	BED COVERS	CURTAINS AND DRAPES	CUSHIONS AND ACCESSORIES	LOOSE COVERS AND TAILORED COVERS	TABLECLOTHS/COVERS	UPHOLSTERY	OTHER
NATURAL FIBERS							
COTTON	✓△	✓	✓	100% cotton	✓	100% for very light use otherwise n/r	
LINEN	✓	✓	✓	as linen/cotton union	✓	100% for very light use otherwise n/r	
SILK	✓	✓	✓		✓	100% for very light use otherwise n/r	
WOOL	✓	✓	✓		✓	✓	
SYNTHETIC FIBERS							
ACETATE	✓	✓	✓	n/r	✓	n/r	
ACRYLIC (Orlon, Verel)	✓	✓	✓	n/r	✓	✓	
MODACRYLIC (Dynel, Verel)	✓	✓	✓	n/r	✓	✓	Flame-retardant
POLYESTER	✓	✓	✓	n/r	✓	in suitable blend	High flame resistance so suitable for public use
VISCOSE (Rayon)	✓	✓	✓	n/r	✓	✓	Drapes, blinds, etc

Lighting Fixtures

Dimmer switches These simple controls serve as an alternative to domestic light switches. They increase or decrease the level of lighting at the turn of a knob or the touch of a plate. Dimmer switches are also available as multiple units that control several circuits. They have wattage limit, and should not be overloaded with too many fittings. Dimmers provide flexible mood lighting and at the same time are energy-saving.

Downlights Circular light fittings that can be recessed, semirecessed, or ceiling-mounted to throw pools of light onto the surface below, downlights can be fitted with various types of bulbs—flood, spot, or ordinary incandescent. Most downlights are anti-glare.

Fluorescent lights Fluorescents are tubular or circular fittings of various sizes. Slim-line, minature tubes are ideal for concealed lighting. Fluorescent lighting is operated by special controls, which makes fittings bulky and awkward but has the advantage of being long-lasting. The light produced can be cool or warm white. New compact fluorescent lights are energy-saving bulbs designed to fit into conventional lamps. This bulb may require an adaptor, and because it is slightly more bulky than an ordinary bulb, a change of shade may be necessary if it is being fitted into an existing lamp.

Framing projectors These lighting units are a domestic adaptation of theatrical lighting and can be shuttered to provide an accurate beam of light. They are ideal for highlighting pictures or displays.

Incandescent lamps These are conventional filament bulbs, also known as tungsten bulbs. They can be pearlized, plain, or colored and come with bayonet or screw fittings. They give a warmer light than fluorescent lamps.

Neon sculptures or tubes Available in a variety of colors, these can be shaped to form a decorative light or lamp. They can also be shaped to follow contours and used to frame a window or mirror, or outline a handrail or beam.

Reflector bulbs These are incandescent light bulbs with a reflector coating. They are ideal for direct lighting because they give a stronger beam than a conventional bulb for the same wattage. They are available for most fittings. Conventional spotlight bulbs are usually of this type.

Rise-and-fall fittings Designed for ceiling lamp or pendant fittings, these enable the lamp to be moved up and down at will.

Track lighting With track lighting, one electric outlet can supply several fittings, which are plugged into the track. Tracks are most widely used for spotlights, but other lamps can be used if they have the correct plug-in fittings. Tracks can be recessed or surface-mounted, and positioned across the ceiling, down walls, or along woodwork. They can be fixed to form squares, oblongs, and even circles, and the lights can usually be angled in several directions.

Tungsten-halogen lamps Originally developed for car headlights, tungsten-halogen lamps give out a small, concentrated light. They provide very powerful light from very small fittings. They must be handled with care so that the quartz envelope is not damaged. (It is important not to touch the actual bulb with your fingers.) Halogen lamps can be used with dimmer controls, but check with an electrician or lighting expert, because the rated wattage of dimmer equipment must be doubled if low-voltage tungsten-halogen fittings are installed.

Uplights   Uplights throw light upward, providing a dramatic accent light. They can be placed on floors, in among plants, or on shelves.

Wallwashers   These are literally designed to "wash a wall" with light and color and make a room seem much more spacious. They are usually fixed about 3 to 5 feet away from the wall and ceiling-mounted, but they can be placed closer to the wall if you want to use them to illuminate a collection of paintings or other wall decorations. In a large room, several wallwashers will be needed to achieve the correct balance of light.

GLOSSARY

Accent A contrasting color, often provided by accessories, to brighten a decorative scheme, to add interest, or to highlight. Accents may also be used to calm down a garish decor.

Accessory An accessory can be anything from a formally displayed collection to a picture, books, cushions, china and glass, or houseplants. Accessories add interest to a room and can be chosen to soften or emphasize a style. Accessories often provide the color accents in a room.

Adjacent Colors A color-theory term that describes colors found next to each other on a color wheel.

Advancing Colors These are colors that appear to come toward you—strong, warm colors such as red, orange, and yellow.

Alcove A vaulted recess in the wall of a room. An alcove may have an arched or a squared top.

Antiquing A process used to age wood and other surfaces artificially, achieved with paint, glazes, and washes that are then ''distressed'' to give them a worn appearance.

Ball-and-Claw Foot A foot of a piece of furniture or a bathtub designed in the shape of a bird's claw or lion's paw holding a ball between its talons or claws. It was much used in the eighteenth century and later copied by the Victorians.

Baluster An upright often vase-shaped or turned vertical support for a handrail of a staircase or for a table leg. See also *Banister*.

Banister One of the upright supports of a handrail alongside a staircase. Also can be used to mean handrail.

Beading A narrow molding of wood or plaster with a pattern similar to a string of beads used with other molding, on a panel, frame, or a wall, or as part of the decorative molding on furniture. Beading can be rounded, as in round beads, or square or latticed.

Brightness Applied to color, brightness means highly saturated—vivid or strong.

Café Curtains Two or more rows of curtains, suspended one above the other across a window, usually on rods. They were originally seen in French and Belgian cafés, where they provided some privacy but enticed would-be customers with a glimpse of an attractive interior.

Chair Rail Molding running around a dining room at chair-back height. Originally used in Colonial homes to keep the chairs from leaving marks on the walls, today chair rails are decorative, often setting up a *dado* effect whereby the space above the rail is treated one way and that below another.

COLOR BOARD A piece of board with samples of the color components of a decorative scheme attached.

COLOR WHEEL A method of showing the colors of the spectrum and how the three primary colors mix to form secondary and tertiary colors. Colors on one side of the wheel are cool and on the other side warm. The color wheel also demonstrates the relationship between *complementary* colors and *adjacent* colors.

COMBING A painting technique in which a wet layer of paint or *glaze* is run through with the rigid teeth of a comb, to produce a striped effect or to simulate *wood graining*.

COMPLEMENTARY COLORS Pairs of colors that appear opposite each other on the *color wheel*—for example, red and green, of which one is *receding* (cool) and the other *advancing* (warm). If two complementary colors are used in equal proportions, the advancing color will appear to dominate.

CORNICE A decorative horizontal band of plaster, wood, or metal used to trim the top of a wall where it meets the ceiling, or to conceal curtain fixtures or lighting fittings.

CROWN MOLDING A ceiling *relief decoration* that usually surrounds the central light fixture but may be positioned singly or in groups almost anywhere on the bed of the ceiling.

DADO A wall treatment where the lower part is separated from the upper part by a *chair rail* or even a wallpaper border or *frieze*. The lower part is usually created differently from the upper, and is frequently paneled or covered with a heavily textured wall covering.

DRAGGING or DRAGGED PAINTWORK A painting technique used on walls and woodwork, where an almost dry brush is dragged across a surface to texture it.

FRAMING PROJECTOR A lighting device that enables differently sized washes of light to be projected onto desired surfaces or areas of a room.

FRIEZE A horizontal band around the walls of a room, usually positioned below the cornice or ceiling and above a picture rail. The term is also used to describe a narrow strip of wallpaper positioned horizontally around the upper half of walls of a room.

GLAZE The application of a transparent or semitransparent color over another color to enrich and intensify it. Glazing is part of the painting technique of glazing and wiping, where the glaze is applied and then wiped with a cloth or "distressed" with another tool or fabric to create an interesting texture.

GRAINING A painting technique that imitates the grain and knots in wood and is used to make a poor-quality wood appear more expensive or to give another surface, such as heavily textured paper, the appearance of wood. Graining can be achieved in several ways, including *dragging, ragging, combing,* or *scumbling.*

GROUT A material worked into the gaps between tiles to create a flush surface.

HARMONY A mixture of colors that creates a pleasing effect.

HUE Pure color—the attribute of one color that distinguishes it from another color. The colors on the basic *color wheel* (primary, secondary, and tertiary) are hues.

JAMB The side supports and molding of a door, window, or fireplace.

LAMINATE A tough surface material formed by pressing together layers of different substances. It is used to cover countertops and to face furniture and kitchen cabinets.

"LIVE" PLASTER Plaster that has begun to crumble and that breaks up under pressure. The only successful treatment is to cut it out and replaster the place, building it up in layers if necessary.

MARBLING A decorative finish that imitates marble, usually achieved with paint. High-quality marbling can be difficult to distinguish from the real thing. Printed marbled effects are produced on wallpapers and fabrics.

MOIRÉ A wavy texture on fabric, creating a watered effect (also called "watered silk").

MOLDING Decorative plasterwork used on ceilings, woodwork, paneling, or around window frames and doors.

MONOCHROMATIC A term used to describe a color scheme based on different *values* of one color, from light through to very dark.

NEUTRALS Light tones that complement bright colors. The true neutrals are black, white, and gray, but in interior design terms, fawn, beige, off-white, and cream are also described as neutral. Items that take their color from natural sources, such as stone, wood, sand, and slate, are considered neutrals, as are some simple striped and checked patterns.

NEWEL POST The initial upright post of a staircase, usually found at the bottom of a stairs and often on the landings.

PALLADIAN WINDOWS Large, beautiful, arching windows that are often found in post-modern buildings or houses and that often form the centerpieces of the structures.

PIGMENT Coloring matter—the essential ingredient added to paint to obtain the required color.

POINTILLISM A method of designing or painting with dots, usually using the pointed end of an instrument, to suggest form and to produce a soft-focus look.

PRISM A transparent polyhedron with two polygonal faces lying in parallel planes, with the other faces parallelograms, which, when a beam of lights passes through it, breaks it into its component colors. (Light, which appears to be white, can then be seen as being comprised of all colors shown in the *color wheel*.)

RAG ROLLING A painting technique that creates a textured effect by applying a base coat, allowing it to dry, then applying a second coat or *glaze* with crumpled-up rags dipped in color.

RECEDING COLORS Colors that appear to go away from you, creating an impression of space and visually increasing the size of the surface on which they are used, particularly in their palest *values*. Receding colors are from the cool side of the *color wheel*—blue, green, and violet.

RELIEF DECORATION A heavily textured surface where part of the design stands out from the background in relief. Some wall coverings have a relief design and a raised and textured surface. Decorative *moldings* are also known as "relief decoration."

REPRODUCTION Furniture, design, and decoration materials made by contemporary methods and from contemporary materials to an original design from an earlier period. Older styles have been copied in this way since pre-Georgian times, and reproductions of reproductions are frequently found.

SCUMBLING A painting effect used to achieve a

wood graining or *marbling* effect. A scumble glaze is applied over a surface color with a circular motion of the brush. Scumble glaze can be bought ready-made or mixed from artists' oil paint, linseed oil, and turpentine.

SHADE A *hue* that has been mixed with black or gray to deepen or soften it.

SPACE DESIGNER A licensed professional whose role falls somewhere between that of an architect and an interior designer. A space designer can advise on making the best use of your house or apartment and how to make traffic flow within it. He or she can also give suggestions about structural matters, such as removing walls.

SPATTERING A decorative painted finish achieved by splashing colors over a solid-color background. Different colors or different *values* of a color can be used together to create a soft, speckled effect.

SPECTRUM The colors of the rainbow—the pure hues of red, orange, yellow, green, blue, and violet—which are created when light is passed through a *prism*.

SPLIT-COMPLEMENTARY A color *harmony* achieved with three colors—one pure *hue,* together with the two colors that appear on either side of its *complementary* on a *color wheel,* for example, green with red-orange and red-violet or blue with yellow-orange and red-orange.

SPONGING A painting technique used to create a soft texture, achieved by dabbing a top color over a base coat with a natural sea sponge or artificial equivalent. A sponge can also be used to remove partially a still-wet top coat or *glaze.*

STIPPLING A painting technique that creates a slightly speckled texture. The tip of a stiff-bristled stippling or stencil brush is pounded on a wet surface or used to apply a second color.

SURROUND The area around the opening of a fireplace. It is usually made of stone, brick, or cement.

TINT A *hue* that has been mixed with white to lighten it.

TENTING A method of draping a ceiling with fabric, sometimes continuing down the walls.

TONAL VALUE The gradation of one *hue* from light to dark.

TONE A color based on a *hue.*

TROMPE L'OEIL Literally, "fool the eye," this term describes decorative effects that are visually deceptive—for example, a window with a realistic view painted on a windowless wall.

VALANCE An area of fabric used to cover the top of a curtain.

VALUE A term used to describe the light or dark quality of a color.

WOOD GRAINING The natural grain in timber, which can be simulated using painting techniques such as *combing* and *scumbling.*

Index

PHOTO CREDITS

Consumer Reports Books would like to thank the following photographers, architects, and designers for permission to reproduce their work.

Karen Bussolini: page 141; *Motif Designs,* pages 18, 45; *Lyman Goff Architect,* page 22; painted floor by *John Canning* of *Canning and Company,* pages 62, 138; *Signature Kitchen and Bath,* page 77; *Paul Hopper Architect,* page 78.

Randall J. Corcoran: *Jerry Sturm* of *Joncich, Sturm and Associates Architects, Cynthia Scarlata Interior Design,* page 8 (top and bottom), page 19.

Daniel Eifert: pages 25, 128, 148; *Lewis Haller,* pages 60, 61; *Marcia Gewanter,* page 80 (top and bottom), *Edward Cohen Inc.,* page 85.

Esto Photographics/Peter Aaron: page 140; *Jay Walter,* page 68; *Greene and Greene,* page 146; *Veverka Massey,* page 151

Esto Photographics/Mark Darley: pages 31, 154, 158.

Esto Photographics/Scott Frances: *Norma King,* page 67; *Sara Olesker,* page 74 (bottom), *Harriet Levine,* page 136.

Tom Leighton: page 14.

Jeff McNamara: pages 27, 41, 142, 144.

Robert Perron: pages 29, 84, 92; *Noyes Vogt Architects,* page 42; *Guilford Knight Architects,* page 48; *Dan Haslegrave, Strutura,* pages 54, 55; *Ted Pappas,* pages 74 (top), 106, 110; *Linda Banks,* page 137; *Ann Sargent,* page 139.

George Ross/Scot P. Samuelson, AIA: page 107.

Tim Street-Porter: pages 24, 26, 28, 90, 91, 126 (top and bottom), 127, 143, 149, 150, 153, 159.

Paul Warchol: page 156 (top and bottom).

Bryan Whitney: page 147.

Jacket photograph by **Robert Perron,** *Killingworth, Tunney Architects,* courtesy of Hearst Magazines. Additional photography is by **John Heseltine**.